RESTORING WOODEN HOUSES

Restoring Wooden Houses

NIGEL HUTCHINS
and
Donna Farron Hutchins

for Limestone Productions Ltd.

KEY PORTER BOOKS

Contents

Foreword / 8

Introduction / 9

CHAPTER ONE
Tradition and Material / 13

CHAPTER TWO
Philosophy and Approach / 37

CHAPTER THREE
Survey and Assessment / 52

CHAPTER FOUR
Exteriors / 73

CHAPTER FIVE
Interiors / 103

CHAPTER SIX
Finishes / 123

CHAPTER SEVEN
Additions and Landscaping / 148

Glossary / 159

Bibliography / 167

Additional Resources / 169

Further Readings / 171

Index / 175

About the Authors / 176

Foreword

It is not the full bottle of wine that the sommelier's silver tasting-dish delivers to your lips, but a taste … an understanding of the wine at hand. And from it the sommelier determines the fitness of the wine for the table. In a similar manner, Limestone Productions' book *Restoring Wooden Houses* brings us an understanding of the vast knowledge one can gain in the restoration of historic homes. The book, authored by Nigel and Donna Hutchins, is an entry into the mysteries of restoration and an overview of all the concerns about restoring houses.

I remember some 35 years ago when I first became interested in the restoration of homes and furniture and searched about for a guide, a map, a touchstone. Nothing was there, and it took many frustrating years of poking about before I started to understand buildings and their problems, and the many sources of help that were at hand. This book should save you from much of this frustration, for not only does it provide points of departure for learning more about particular restoration problems, it also provides immediate practical advice that can be applied to restoring one's home.

Books can't replace hands-on experience, and other people's experience cannot replace the necessity of gaining your own experience through trial and error. Hopefully mistakes will come without too much pain or expense. No one book can do it all for you.

Use the book's bibliography to find titles that will expand your capabilities. Don't be afraid to buy good tools and learn how to use them — they are your birthright as *homo faber*, the creator. And don't think that there is some set of absolute rules that a restoration must follow. Be guided by safety, by your financial and time capabilities and by your heart. Our architectural heritage was built by the souls of generations past. Add to it, and find joy in your place in the lineage of people who care about the very best that is within us.

Richard O. Byrne
Staunton, Virginia

Introduction

With this volume, Limestone Productions Ltd. brings closure to the *Restoring Houses* trilogy. This began in 1981, with the publication of *Restoring Old Houses,* and continued two years later with the release of *Restoring Houses of Brick and Stone.* At last we complete the cycle with an examination of the wooden house. In *Restoring Wooden Houses* we are not dealing with the "great house" of North America, but with the thousands of individual houses that were home to what used to be termed the middle class. This is the house of the "everyman."

Limestone Productions Ltd.

To restore a house is not an exercise of playing Mr. or Mrs. Fix-it, armed with hammer and saw. It is a philosophy that marries many disciplines. Technical expertise is required — that of everything from carpenter to mason, from roofer to painter. The philosophical disciplines require that you stand back and look at another person's house with sympathetic objectivity. Your present involvement in that house makes you a part of the house's history, for whatever time you may enjoy being the inhabitants of it.

The process of preservation is a fortunate side-effect of North America's dwindling resources. The mass popularity of fixing old things — the commercialization of it — has in many ways changed the focus of the "preservation movement." Twenty years ago one could still find houses that were architecturally intact but had suffered years of neglect. This neglect, while negative in itself, was often ideal to the individual who wished to restore. Any changes were easily dealt with because fine period detailing (such as molding) had been left intact. Now, with the popularization of preservation, we find physical neglect being overtaken by wanton ignorance, where yesterday's domestic architectural heritage takes a back seat to today's popular taste. It is hoped that this book will serve as a guide to those who are sincere in their approach to the period home. This is not a technical manual, but more of a caution on how "not to do it," and how to embrace a judicious and humane process.

My many associates have brought with them their years of experience. I would like to thank my partner and co-author Donna Farron, with whom I have shared many horrible and wonderful experiences in the cause of rural and architectural preservation. Brent McGillivray's excellent drawings illustrate what words often cannot explain. The photographs contributed by Danny Burke and Richard O. Byrne add to the tapestry of talents and insights that we hope you will treasure. Thanks to my editorial partners, Patrick Crean and Mary Ann McCutcheon, and Anna Porter, for her ongoing support and patience. My thanks to those people and to all who have helped in the completion of this project.

Nigel Hutchins

Until I met Nigel I had always admired older buildings from afar. Growing up in a large brick house of the 1940s era, in Toronto, I did not really comprehend the term "old house." My first date with Nigel seemed quite novel, but was to become somewhat typical: hurling some old rubber boots (a staple if you live in the country) into the backseat of his old Volvo, he took me off to look at an abandoned 1830 house in Eastern Ontario. The scent of the wet pine, the vast array of colorful wildflowers and the mystery of this abandoned dwelling all combined to capture my interest. What finally entrenched me, however, was the muck, as we returned to the car. Tromping far ahead of me, Nigel never noticed that I was stuck in the middle of an unplowed field. The rather large boots that I had been wearing began to sink deeper into the soil, and I was immobilized. With all the chivalry of an eighteenth-century gent he responded to my cries of distress and returned to carry me back to the vehicle, the rubber boots left behind. Needless to say, I was enraptured. Of course, one of my first presents from him was a pair of black rubber boots that fit.

Wooden houses carry a special air of romanticism. From the cozy log house to the salty cape house of coastal New England to the charm of a Victorian clapboard decorated with ornate gingerbread — each has its story and allure. I particularly love the simplicity and texture of a log house with painted interior. Houses of this era seem to be asking you to bring the joys of the outside in. Dried herbs and flowers hanging from beams, pots of preserves filling the house with tantalizing aromas, stacks of dried wood sitting outside the summer kitchen, jugs of apple cider crushed from fresh, hand-picked fruit. That is surely a bit of heaven. Modern homes, wonderful as some of them are, do not offer me the same inspiration. I guess that walk through a farmer's field 25 years ago left quite an impression.

Donna Farron Hutchins

Acknowledgments

The following people have made their own unique contributions to the field of preservation and design. The commitment and knowledge of Peter John Stokes, Blake McKendry, Phil Shackleton, John Player, William Watson, Martin Weil, Martin Weaver, the late Ann Faulkner, R.A.J. Phillips, Jacques Dalibard, and Francois Barbeau have been an inspiration.

Others continue to keep the practice of this sometimes difficult profession alive: Tony Jenkins, James Coligan, Mel Shakespeare, Chris Blott and Scott Little.

Our personal projects could never have been attempted without the skill and craftsmanship of Paul Croteau, Glenn Billings and Graham Thomas.

Support comes in diverse ways. Thank you to Jim Hunter (Black Creek Pioneer Village), Rita Russell and Susan Hughes (Tormorden Mills Heritage Museum), Steichen Lab, Pat Johnson, Florence Newell, Pat and Harve Malcolm, Zena and Jean Paul Laroche, Gary Nichol, Ken and Doris Lawless, Edith and Bob Lenz, Danny Burke, Jim and Leona Armstrong, Stan and Jean Slivinski, Winnifred Hutchins, Leslie and Betty Hutchins and our sons Dylan and Jesse.

CHAPTER ONE

Tradition and Material

Before the Europeans arrived in the New World, Natives had already perfected the use of indigenous materials in wood structures. The Native longhouse, which combined wood framing with animal hides, was a precursor to the first wooden homes of the colonists. Three hundred years later the well-known rock and roll pioneer, Chuck Berry, referred to a log cabin made of earth and wood belonging to a fellow named "Johnny-be-Good." This cabin in the Appalachians was probably created from wattle and daub. Johnny did what humans have done throughout time: he made use of the resources that were available to him. The settlers who arrived on this continent brought with them European traditions and technology. The use of local materials and traditional building techniques laid the foundation for North American domestic architecture. It is important to understand how this came about.

The wattle and daub structure is a prime example of how to make use of what is available. It consists of small saplings woven together in an almost basket-like weave, and then coated with mud, clay or similar material. In England this coating was known as "clob," consisting of a mixture of horse manure with clay and straw, which was then smeared over a patchwork quilt of saplings. This created a parging that held the whole thing together. In point of fact you ended up with a house made of wood, combined with masonry. This marrying of materials can be traced through European and into North American construction. The seventeenth-century settlement in Jamestown, Virginia, is a perfect example of the use of timber framing combined with a mud or clay infill.

Early Spanish settlement of the New World in the same period followed the same dictates. The Spanish tradition of employing masonry in architecture can be seen in the buildings of their colonies, which used

Wattle and daub infill in a Pilgrim house of the late seventeenth century in Jamestown, Virginia.

A traditional longhouse.

French, English and American Decorative Styles, 1500–1860

	FRANCE		ENGLAND		AMERICA
Years	Reign	Style	Reign	Style	Style
1500	Louis XII–Henri III 1498–1589	Renaissance	Henri VII– Elizabeth 1st 1485–1603	Tudor Elizabethan	
1600					
1625	Henri IV 1589–1610	Louis XIII	The Stuarts & Commonwealth 1603–1688	Jacobean Cromwellian Charles II	
1650	Louis XIII 1610–1643				
1675	Louis XIV 1643–1715	Louis XIV	William & Mary 1689–1702	William & Mary	William & Mary 1700–1725
1700	Regency	Régence	Anne	Queen Anne	Queen Anne
1725	1715–1722		1702–1714		1725–1750
1730					
1750	Louis XV 1722-1774	Louis XV	Early Georgian 1714–1760	Chippendale	Chippendale
1775	Louis XVI 1774–1792 Directory 1795–1799	Louis XVI Directoire	Late Georgian 1760–1830	c. 1749–1779 Adam c. 1760–1792 Hepplewhite c. 1785–1790	1760–1790 Hepplewhite 1790–1810
1800	Consulate & 1st Empire 1799–1814	First Empire		Sheraton c. 1785–1806	Sheraton 1790–1818
1825	Louis XVIII 1815–1824 Charles X 1824–1830 Louis-Philippe 1830–1848	Restauration Louis-Philippe	Victoria 1837–1901	Regency 1795–1837 Early Victorian	Regency 1820–1840 c. 1837
1850	Napoleon III 1852–1870	Second Empire		Late Victorian c. 1851	

Source: Jean Palardy, *The Furniture of French Canada*. Toronto: Macmillan, 1963.

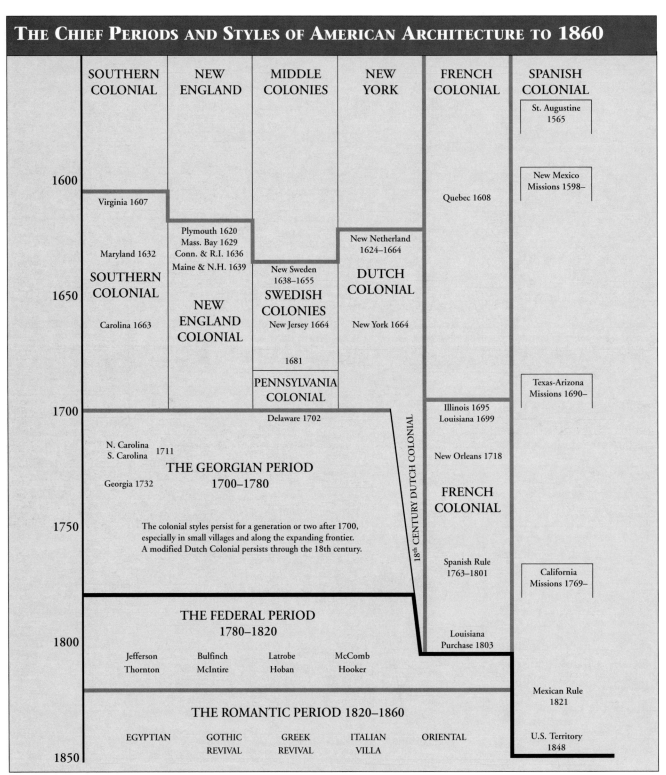

THE CHIEF PERIODS AND STYLES OF AMERICAN ARCHITECTURE TO 1860

SOUTHERN COLONIAL	NEW ENGLAND	MIDDLE COLONIES	NEW YORK	FRENCH COLONIAL	SPANISH COLONIAL
					St. Augustine 1565

1600

Virginia 1607

Quebec 1608

New Mexico Missions 1598–

Maryland 1632

Plymouth 1620
Mass. Bay 1629
Conn. & R.I. 1636
Maine & N.H. 1639

New Netherland 1624–1664

SOUTHERN COLONIAL

New Sweden 1638–1655

DUTCH COLONIAL

1650

Carolina 1663

NEW ENGLAND COLONIAL

SWEDISH COLONIES
New Jersey 1664

New York 1664

1681

PENNSYLVANIA COLONIAL

Texas-Arizona Missions 1690–

1700

Delaware 1702

Illinois 1695
Louisiana 1699

N. Carolina
S. Carolina   1711

THE GEORGIAN PERIOD
1700–1780

New Orleans 1718

Georgia 1732

FRENCH COLONIAL

1750

The colonial styles persist for a generation or two after 1700,
especially in small villages and along the expanding frontier.
A modified Dutch Colonial persists through the 18th century.

Spanish Rule
1763–1801

California Missions 1769–

18th CENTURY DUTCH COLONIAL

THE FEDERAL PERIOD
1780–1820

Louisiana Purchase 1803

1800

| Jefferson | Bulfinch | Latrobe | McComb |
| Thornton | McIntire | Hoban | Hooker |

Mexican Rule 1821

THE ROMANTIC PERIOD 1820–1860

| EGYPTIAN | GOTHIC REVIVAL | GREEK REVIVAL | ITALIAN VILLA | ORIENTAL |

U.S. Territory 1848

1850

Source: Hugh Morrison, *Early American Architecture.* New York: Oxford University Press, 1981.

materials readily available (such as mud and straw) for adobe structures that employed timbers as structural elements and for roof framing. Unfortunately, adobe, like wattle and daub, is very susceptible to deterioration. Unless there is ongoing maintenance provided, a breakdown of the material occurs very quickly and the longevity of the house doesn't exceed 25 to 30 years.

Early construction was born of three considerations: the material available, the technology that could lend shape to that material and the inherent tradition of building. When the first settlers arrived on the shores of the Eastern Seaboard they had to immediately create shelter-giving structures for survival. The material that was most readily available and easiest to work with was, of course, wood. The primeval forests of North America that surrounded the early settlers consisted of two types of trees: the hardwood (broad-leaved trees such as oak, walnut, mahogany, maple, butternut and black walnut); and the softwood (coniferous trees such as pine, spruce and redwood). Cedar, cherry, birch, hemlock and ash were also widely used. Pine was most commonly used because it was soft and easy to work with. The settlers had the technical knowledge of how to make use of these massive timbers.

Architectural evidence shows that timber framing was in use throughout France and England in early Anglo-Saxon times. These timber-framed buildings can be traced back to the seventh century in England, France and Norway. Although this text deals with the house of the everyman, it is interesting to hear the description of the house of Lambert of Ardens in Flanders. It is a wooden tower house, built on top of a mountain by a carpenter, Louis de Bourbourg.

ABOVE & FOLLOWING PAGE
French timber-framing methods.

FRAMING CHART

This shows the three general stages as well as the transitional periods.

1. Timber framing	1600–1830
2. Braced framing	1770–1830
3. Balloon framing (with some bracing)	1830–1880
4. Balloon framing (all nails)	1880–1925
5. Western framing or contemporary framing	1925–present

The first ... storey were cellars and granaries. In the storey above were the dwelling ... rooms of the residents.... Adjoining this was a private room ... where ... they used to have a fire. In the upper storey ... were garret rooms.... High up on the east side of the house ... was the chapel, which was made like the tabernacle of Solomon in its ceiling and painting.

MARGARET WOOD, FROM THE ENGLISH MEDIEVAL HOUSE

House-building with wood in North America has evolved through three general historical stages. First, the timber-frame unit, which was basically a handmade house. The timbers were hewn and jointed together with pins. The simplicity of this technology was based on necessity, for nails were not readily accessible, nor were large quantities of milled lumber. This method of construction took place in early settlements until the 1830s. Then, as the first-cut forests rapidly disappeared, balloon framing came into being. By the early 1900s we have examples of contemporary framing methods, often referred to as Western framing.

It is helpful to look at these styles more closely if we are to understand the evolution of wooden house-building in North America.

The timber-frame house was an actual framework made of timbers. The frame was divided into 10 units. The main units, the **sills,** rested on top of a foundation wall and carried the main frame. The **posts** were the upright vertical supports. The **girts** were the main horizontal supports, carrying the second floor. They were morticed into the posts. The **summer beam** was a large, heavy beam spanning the middle of a large room, usually from end girt to chimney girt. It was often the biggest beam in the house. **Joists** were the smaller beams that carried the floorboards. They ran across the house in two spans, from girt to summer beam and from summer beam to rear girt. Their ends rested in notches. The **plates** were the horizontal timbers at the top of the wall, on top of which the rafters rested. The **rafters** were the slanting beams supporting the pitched roof. There were two types of these: the "principal" rafters, usually heavy timbers over the posts, and common timbers, which were the lighter timbers, spaced between the principal rafters. **Purlins** were horizontal beams set between principal rafters at one or more levels between plate and ridge plate. Often the rafters met in lap joints, and sometimes there was a ridge pole (something we would normally use today). Diagonal bracing was then used for wind and collars.

The timber frame was then sheathed. **Sheathing** is a layer of thin planks applied to the framework. **Siding** would then be applied to the sheathing. Clapboard siding was commonly used (a name derived from the German klapholz, meaning barrel stave). It traditionally consisted of thin, wedge-shaped boards, about five inches wide and four to six feet long — enough to cross three or four studs. They would be split and rivened, rather than sawed, so that in fact they resembled an ordinary cut plank, and they would be cut again. They were split into quarters and eighths, and so produced a number of

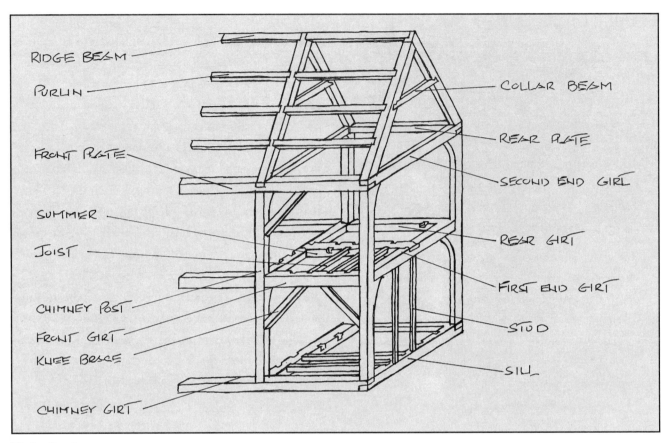

RIDGE BEAM
PURLIN
COLLAR BEAM
FRONT PLATE
REAR PLATE
SECOND END GIRT
SUMMER
JOIST
REAR GIRT
CHIMNEY POST
FIRST END GIRT
FRONT GIRT
KNEE BRACE
STUD
SILL
CHIMNEY GIRT

Timber framing.

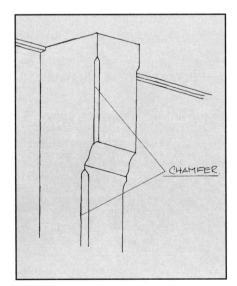

CHAMFER

Chamfer.

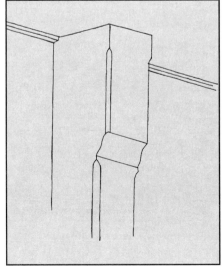

Post bracket.

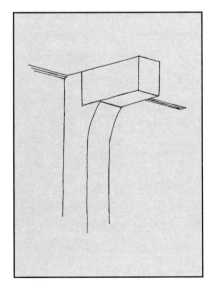

Post flare.

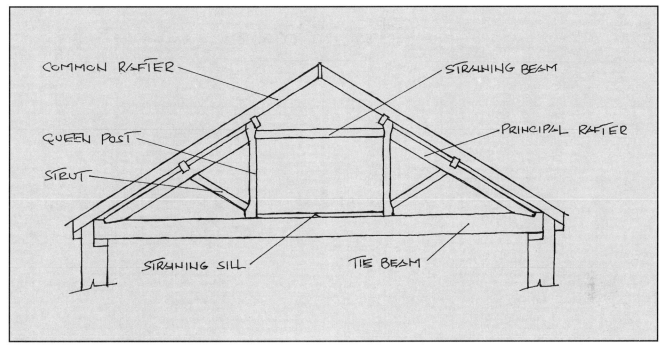

Queen post truss.

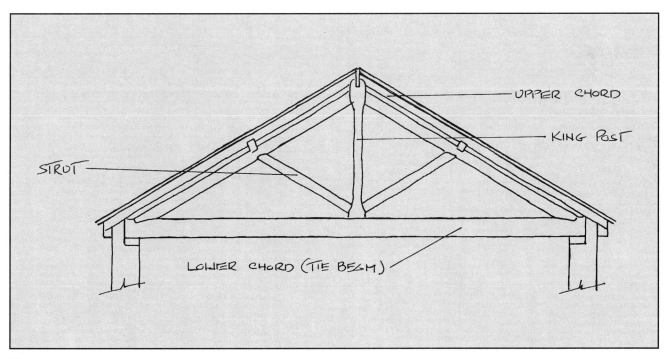

King post truss.

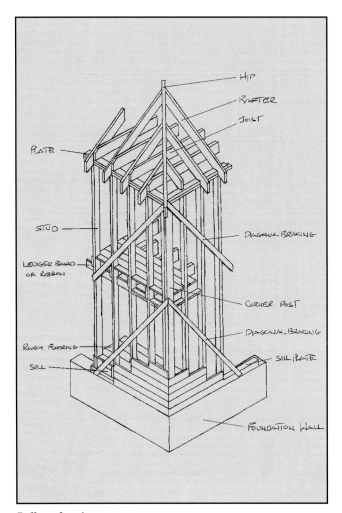

Labels on left diagram (Balloon framing):
HIP
RAFTER
JOIST
PLATE
STUD
LEDGER BOARD OR RIBBON
ROUGH FLOORING
SILL
DIAGONAL BRACING
CORNER POST
DIAGONAL BRACING
SILL PLATE
FOUNDATION WALL

Balloon framing.

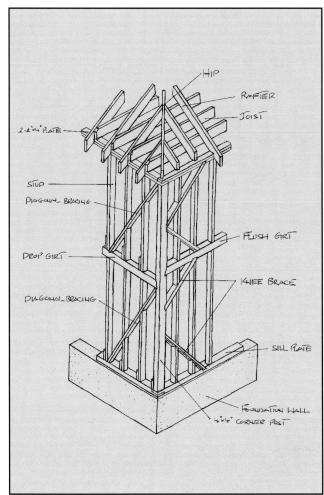

Labels on right diagram (Braced framing):
HIP
RAFTER
JOIST
2×4" PLATE
STUD
DIAGONAL BRACING
DROP GIRT
DIAGONAL BRACING
FLUSH GIRT
KNEE BRACE
SILL PLATE
FOUNDATION WALL
4×4" CORNER POST

Braced framing.

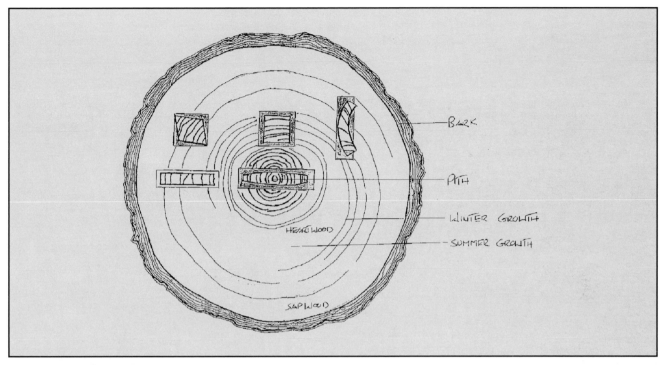

Section of a tree for board cutting.

Late 19th-century lumbering.

wedge-shaped pieces about half an inch thick, tapered to a feather edge. Exterior walls could also be covered with shingles, which were used on walls as well as roofs. The shingles would be hand-riven and split with a froe. If you can still find them on an exterior you will notice that they are of various dimensions, crude and thick, compared to modern mill-cut shingles.

It must be remembered that until the late eighteenth century, all of the aforementioned construction was done by hand. Samuel Strickland, a lumberman on the Trent River in Ontario, has left us a firsthand account of cutting and squaring operations in about 1850.

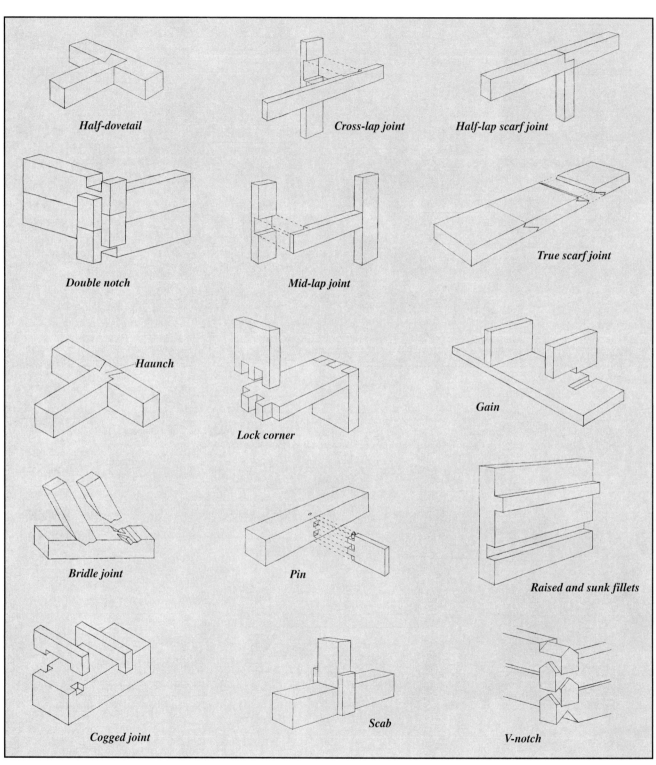

Half-dovetail

Cross-lap joint

Half-lap scarf joint

Double notch

Mid-lap joint

True scarf joint

Haunch

Lock corner

Gain

Bridle joint

Pin

Raised and sunk fillets

Cogged joint

Scab

V-notch

Various types of joints.

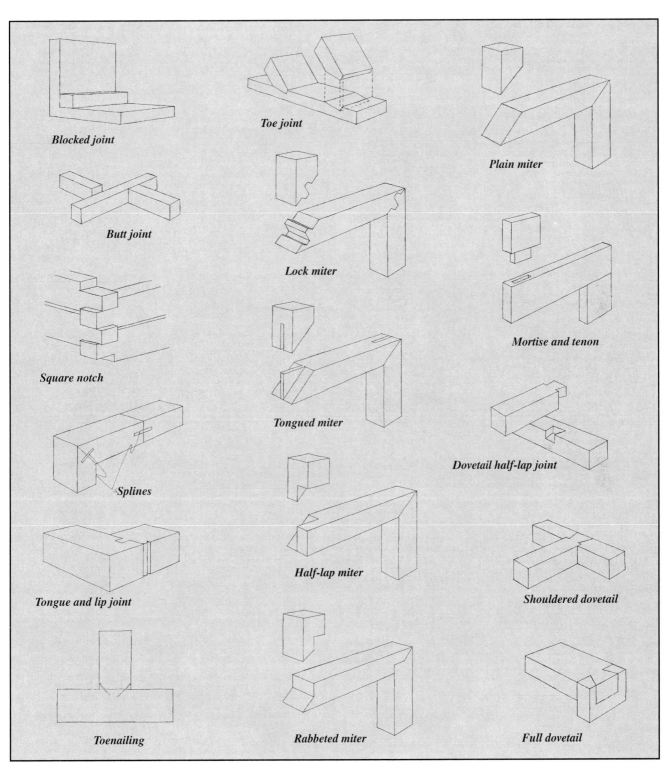

Blocked joint

Toe joint

Plain miter

Butt joint

Lock miter

Mortise and tenon

Square notch

Tongued miter

Dovetail half-lap joint

Splines

Tongue and lip joint

Half-lap miter

Shouldered dovetail

Toenailing

Rabbeted miter

Full dovetail

Various types of joints.

The workmen are divided into gangs. A gang of men cut down the trees, taking care to throw small trees, called bedding timbers, across the path the tree will fall, for the purpose of keeping it from freezing to the ground or endangering the edge of the workmen's axes against stones or earth. This plan has another advantage, for in the deep snow it greatly facilitates the loading of the timber. As soon as the tree is felled, a person, called a liner, rosses and lines the tree on each side and the axe-men cut the top of the trees off, at the length determined on by the liner: they also square the butt-end of the stick, leaving a sort of rough tenon with a mortice-hole through it at both ends of the timber, which are made on purpose to pass the withes through when rafting them. The tree is now ready for the hewer's gang, which generally consists of the hewer and three, or at most four, axe-men, all of whom stand on the prostrate trunk of the tree, except the hewer.

A log house in the French tradition, from Quebec, circa 1820.

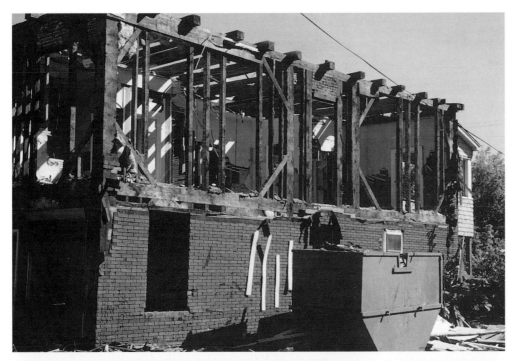

LEFT & BELOW
**A braced-frame house,
showing numeric markings
of its major components.**

One man then cuts a row of notches as deep into the side of the tree as the line-mark will allow, or nearly so, between two and three feet apart; a second splits the blocks off between the notches; and the third scores the rough surface, taking care not to cut too deep. The hewer then follows with his broad axe, and cleans off all the inequalities left by the scorers.

A second gang, similar to the first, only one axeman less, now takes possession of the tree, which has been already squared on its two sides by the first gang. The tree is now turned down upon one of its hewn faces, measured off, and lined on both outside edges; and the same process is gone through, as before described, which finishes the operation of "making," as the lumber men term squaring the timber.

The very earliest planks were cut from logs using pit saws. In the process, a pit was dug in the earth and a frame erected over the pit to hold the huge pit-saw blade. The long timbers, previously squared by a broad axe, were placed over it one at a time. The sawyer stood on top and guided the cutting of the timber from end to end. The actual movement was provided by those known as the pit men down below. Besides the fact that this was an extremely laborious process, the men in the pit were constantly showered with sawdust. This made pit sawing a costly and labor-intensive operation. One can imagine how the introduction of the sawmill, in the early 1800s, was truly welcomed. This was an invention born in the mid 1500s in Europe, although the practice was not widely known in England until the late 1600s. The first sash sawmills were modified pit saws, up-and-down affairs driven by water. The sawmills were wholly dependent upon the availability of fast-rushing water that could be dammed and harnessed for their power.

There is documentation of pit saws and gang saws (a series of upright saws) in use throughout North America from the early nineteenth century, and a sawmill was documented in North Berwick, Maine, as early as 1650. In 1831, in what is now known as Bedford Mills, Ontario, Benjamin Tett entered the sawmill business. As James T. Wills relates in *Antiques* magazine,

[Tett] took over a small existing sawmill and began to produce planks and deals for the local market using a single upright muley saw ... [However, he] could not keep pace with demand, and he had to expand as rapidly as possible.... And still he was behind....

In the French settlements of North America, also called New France, traditional framing techniques did not gel with the weather of the New World. The *maison au columbage* style can be seen as a descendant of the medieval half-timbered house of Northwestern Europe. It had a wooden frame with upright studs or posts in the walls, and the intervening space was then filled with stone and mortar. This was termed *columbage pierroté*, and examples of the technique are evident in Normandy and elsewhere in France. Half-timbered buildings were common in eighteenth-century Louisbourg (a French fortress on the northern coast of Nova Scotia) and were also employed throughout New France. The infill in the timber framing was stone, mud or clay. A similar fill, sandwiched between parallel walls or boards, made up the walls of the buildings at the Ste. Marie Among the Hurons in Ontario. Protective boarding, or the sheathing that one would see in New England over the stone walls in the timber framing, appeared at a much later date. In Quebec, these half-timbered buildings disappeared slowly in the eighteenth century due to the rigorous climate. However, it is important to remember that in

ABOVE & LEFT

A one-and-a-half-storey clapboard house, showing interior framing with exterior clapboard.

Wood is used to create the visual effect of a stone house.

A plank house, parged and scored to look like ashlar.

framing techniques, as in all matters of style and construction, one era does not abruptly end and another begin. All domestic architecture was, and is, transitional. In fact, one can find combinations of timber-framing techniques and balloon or braced framing used right up until the early twentieth century throughout New England and Eastern and Western Ontario.

As the inhabitants of New France became more acclimatized and accustomed to the availability of massive amounts of wood, a new technique of building was created, termed *piece sur piece*. This evolution from the *columbage* frame was quite basic. The stone and mortar fill between the upright posts was replaced with wood. This meant that an entire wall of vertical posts would rest on two sides or be fully squared. *Piece sur piece* was popular because it was superior to *columbage* and it wove vertical timbers. Therefore, it offered good drainage and good insulation, and the chinking of moss or cedar would not fall out with the change in temperature. *Piece sur piece* wall shrinkage would cause these squared walls to settle without being dislodged. With the ever-changing temperatures, the material would only get tighter. The *en columbage* method of building can be found anywhere that French settlement took place in North America, showing once again how tradition would determine the building styles. An example is the Magnolia Mount Plantation house in Baton Rouge, Louisiana. As H. Parrot Bacon wrote in *Antiques*:

> The entire house is constructed of columbage — half-timber with laths covered with a mixture of mud, Spanish moss, and animal hair — and sometimes in the late nineteenth or early twentieth century all the columbage, inside and out, was covered with narrow beaded boards.

Original photographic documentation is invaluable in the restoration process.

In timber framing, the framework is an independent and secure entity. In balloon framing, the vulnerable framework requires sheathing and cladding, which are attached with nails for structural integrity. Balloon framing was invented by George Washington Snow of Chicago. It was born of the need to find a way of building cheap, efficient houses with the wood that was available. As Dr. Paul E. Sprague notes in *Technology of Historic American Buildings*,

> *Snow's experiment in building took place in 1832 and was quickly given the apparently derisive name of "balloon" construction, presumably by persons who expected his lightly built structure to be blown away in the first windstorm.*

The earliest balloon frames, as in Snow's invention, still employed some of the techniques of timber-framed building or brace-framed building. This referred specifically to the large sill areas where mortice-and-tenoning was still used, while the material in the rest of the structure was of lesser dimensions.

Of prime interest to the preservationist is the fact that up until the late 1950s, wood materials held their dimensions; for example, the two-by-four was two inches by four inches. Although today the term two-by-four is still used, the dimensions are much less than the name would indicate. This results in houses of less sound structure, in preservationist terms, than the earlier houses.

A cottage constructed in the balloon-frame method was displayed at the Paris Exhibit of 1867. It was built in Chicago and shipped prefabricated. A description of the construction of such a cottage, by Dr. Paul E. Sprague, follows:

THE JAMES C. HOLMES HOUSE

As indicated by the ambitious work schedule of the J.C. Holmes timber-frame house in 1869, balloon framing and the Industrial Revolution were more than welcome.

Jan. 6–Feb. 20, 1869	Lumber and shingles redied; millwork ordered
Feb. 10–Mar. 2	Stone quarried and hauled
Mar. 4–Apr. 10	Windows prepared
Apr. 14–24	Frame hewn
Apr. 30–May 7	Cellar excavated
May 10–27	Foundation laid up
May 28–29	Frame raised
June 2–7	Siding put up
June 8–11	Roofing laid
June 12–16	Flooring laid; exteriors painted
June 17	Bench moved inside; stairs built
June 18–21	Cellar plastered
June 19–21	Partitions built
June 22–28	Base and casings installed
June 26–July 9	Lathing nailed up
July 26–28	Chimney built
Aug. 2–7	House plastered

Workers: James C. Holmes, Horace Holmes, Arthur Holmes, Mary Holmes, Judson Winans, Everett Herdman, German Baldwin, Augustus Baldwin, Charles Tyler, John Goodenough, Denton Salisbury, William O. Ashley, Carlos Ashley, Myron Hubbard

When no foundation ... has been laid, the sills are placed upon cedar posts ... and well pinned. Both the studding and joists are framed into the sills.... At the corners of the building two or three studs are placed together ... spiked together and to the sills. The rafters are framed so as to bear laterally upon the wall plates.... The entire outside of the studding and rafters is covered with common boards ... well nailed down ... then covered with siding.... Floors are laid upon the joists ... nailed down ... [and] inside partitions are set upon the floor ... The lathing and plastering follows....

As this type of construction grew more widespread, the technique itself evolved. By the end of the First World War a new form of construction — born from the initial balloon frame, and called "Western frame construction" — had evolved. This is basically the same type of framing construction we use today for domestic dwellings.

Log Buildings

Log buildings are a primitive form of timber-frame building. Their evolution parallels other forms of timber framing, both in Europe (log buildings are found throughout Northern Continental Europe) and in domestic settlements of the New World. The primeval forests of North America made log buildings a logical, simple and natural form of habitation.

The log house is basically a system in which logs act as both the inner and the outer walls of a structure. The outer walls, combined with the rafter system, are similar to those employed in a timber-framed building. The logs are joined on the corners with different types of notches — dovetails, saddle notches, lap notches. Windows and

A restored 19th-century log house.

doors are then cut out of the logs after they are erected; chinking or masonry material is then applied between the logs. Traditionally, chinking might consist of moss, clay or a mixture of both to weathertight the joints between the logs that lie on top of each other. The advantages of a log house are obvious: they were simple, economical, quick and offered a cozy and warm shelter for the winter. Many of the settlers made do with their shanty or log house before they could erect a more refined dwelling.

Although log houses were a rudimentary form of shelter, many a refinement of the log house did, on occasion, take place. With very little change to the building techniques originally used, log houses evolved into large, two-storey or one-and-a-half-storey houses. They can be found throughout the Southern and Northeastern United States and Canada. In fact, they are found throughout all North American settlements where trees suitable for the dimensions needed could be found.

While initially the New World settlers used the immediately available materials, it is interesting to reflect on the fact that wherever the tradition of building was practiced using European styles and methods, there seemed also to be an air of New World liberalism and simplicity. Colonial architecture is succinctly summed up, for any student of North American architecture and furnishings, by Hugh Morrison in his book *Early American Architecture*:

> *Simplicity and practicality are the keynotes of the Colonial Style. Although building was a direct outgrowth of urgent and practical necessities, there was little time or money for elaboration or ornamentation. These houses have an indigenous flavor, a native quality that makes them seem permanent rather than period pieces.*

LEFT

*The marriage of today's lifestyle to the history of
the house makes for a successful project.*

BELOW

*This 1907 photo gives us a great glimpse of early
plumbing. Note pump and stand in background.*

*Often outbuildings
were erected in a
similar fashion as
the main house.*

The exuberance of yesterday's craftspeople is an ongoing delight to today's preservationist.

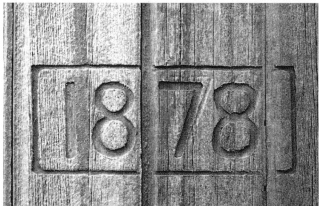

This house is easy to date.

CHAPTER TWO

Philosophy and Approach

Why does one buy an older house? Perhaps the brand-new home in the suburbs is not your taste. Or, due to limited funds, you may have decided that it will be cheaper for out-of-pocket costs to fix up an old house, doing it bit by bit. You may be looking for a home tailored to meet your needs, and a modern custom-built house is cost-prohibitive. Or perhaps the idea of preserving and enjoying a home with maturity and history has lured you into the restoration process.

The mass popularity of fixing old things has presented a new challenge for the preservation movement. Twenty years ago one could readily find houses that were in their original architectural state. Today, overzealous renovators have, in a lot of cases, removed or damaged important elements to such an extent that restoration is almost impossible. This also creates a financial quandary because too much money has already been spent (albeit without care) and so the market value of the property will not often warrant further expense.

This book is not a technical step-by-step manual. It is, however, a challenging statement to guide the preservationist in conserving the fabric and essence of the physical history of the house. The two main methods of refurbishing an old house are reconstruction and historic rehabilitation.

Reconstruction, a process that involves removing large sections of the original fabric of the house and rebuilding it to a contemporary state, is to be discouraged. We would not actively suggest such an arduous process unless a great deal of the house's original fabric is in poor condition, or has been so badly altered that it does not allow for restoration.

Historical rehabilitation is probably the method that most people use today. This employs various elements within the house in a manner that stays true to their original use. In this scenario the layout is maintained as much as possible, and the details of moldings, doorways, etc., are within the configurations of the house as it was built, yet conducive to today's lifestyle. In making this choice, the terms *preservation* and *recycling* marry. Why destroy an element of the past that is reusable? This question is at the center of the preservation process.

To restore a house completely, and I use this term in the clinical sense, is usually beyond the practical and economic means of most people. However, it is the ultimate way to deal with and live in an old house. If you choose to pursue this method, you will find that it is completely satisfying, extremely frustrating, and everything in between. It will challenge you to go to the Nth degree, to find the exact type of hardware that was used originally, the exact tooling on the plaster work, the exact type of paint surfaces, etc.

When you are restoring to a particular era, it is important to understand the evolution of the house. For example, the earliest period (represented by a house built in 1770) may not have been architecturally the most interesting. If you find a 1770 house with an 1830 renovation, it might be far more interesting (not only to you as the inhabitant, but in terms of architectural preservation) to choose the later date as your restoration guide. These are important things to consider. It is rarely worth taking anything decent down just because it is not of the right period. In a private preservation project this not only betrays the history of the house, but is also very uneconomical.

Upon buying an old house, it is very important to ascertain why you have purchased it. Researching the house's history is an important process. Wherever possible, gather information. Talk to neighbors and historical societies or organizations; look at the local

Exterior living spaces are equally important to those inside the walls.

town register, insurance maps and tax assessment rolls. These are all places where one can trace the history of the house and the community. Even if you don't find much specific information about your house, you will find helpful details of houses that were of similar date and architectural styling. It is also helpful to be aware of fashion styles found in books, building manuals, etc., and to look at other domestic architecture from the period in which the house was originally built.

The three approaches to actually restoring a house on a personal level are the personal time-plan method, the self-contractor method and the contractor method.

With the first method your involvement is close and immediate. You control the pace of work, you act as your own designer and consultant. The advantage here is that you are usually living in the house and are aware of the daily changes in your uses of the house, and in the evolution of the house's process. Although it is terribly hard on one's emotional and physical well-being, it's a relatively cost-effective method, particularly if you possess any skills in the preservation trades. This is an in-depth way of finding out what the house may reveal about its history and transformations. The disadvantage is that often the bank manager will not respond favorably to this non-traditional approach and therefore mortgage draws may be delayed or stopped. Your insurance rates may increase as well. You must inquire about the bank's support before you begin.

If you decide to act as the contractor, you will save 10 to 20 percent of the contract fee. However, you will have to be on-site most of the time, and when you are not working you may not be generating the dollars that may be needed for completion of the project. Decisions have to be made, often on the spur of the moment. If you are in charge of the project and you happen to be away, then you will come head to head with long delays

Outstanding neo-Gothic bargeboard.

Period gardens are an integral part of the restoration process.

A charming mid-19th-century clapboard house.

and distraught tradespeople. They have better things to do with their time than waste hours waiting for your approval on some matter. You may find that unless you can be there, you will find it hard to keep the sub-contractors committed to your project. Many people believe the myth that they can work at a full-time job (lawyer, doctor, salesman, whatever) and then come home and restore their house. In some very exceptional cases this may be true. However, it is somewhat shortsighted to take for granted the expertise and knowledge of those who have spent their careers working in specific preservation trades. You cannot pick up the breadth of their experience overnight, or by reading books like this one. Be realistic at the onset of the project.

The contractor method can be the least stressful in most cases. You basically list your requirements, design proposals and form an agreement with a contractor who will carry out your wishes. This is theoretically the most efficient way of completing the project; however, the rigidity of the process sometimes lacks the degree of flexibility that preservation requires. You must have a comfortable alliance with the contractor in order for this method to be successful.

Before you embark on this voyage, take a good look at your own particular lifestyle. Although the home is new to you, it has felt the impact of numerous inhabitants through the years, each with his or her own unique manner of living. How you live today is extremely important. Look at your technical, personal and practical needs, and incorporate them into the process.

Before you commit to anyone, insist on seeing samples of their work. They should have reasonable credit references and referrals from former clients. One thing I wish to warn you of is that you should not

necessarily choose the lowest bid. The time and money spent on choosing someone who really understands the type of building that you own will prove to be cost-effective. Your tradespeople will be spending a lot of time with you. It is important for everyone to develop a trusting relationship. Have a clear understanding between everyone involved on how you will approach and deal with problems and other matters that arise.

The architect, or consultant, may end up playing the role of mentor for you. Preservation is very much a team effort and often the people involved will be unaware of each other's skills and knowledge. For example, an engineer who specializes in contemporary structures may not be aware of the unique problems you may find in a certain type of timber-framed building. Therefore, it is important to consult and work in unison with this engineer and the people actually working on the building, so that there is a meeting of the minds. When this occurs problems are usually successfully solved.

If employing an architect or designer, remember that the building is already built, and you have bought it because of the appeal that it has for you. If an addition is to be put on, then perhaps the designer or architect can field some visual ideas — but he or she must remember that preservation is a process of preserving what someone else has already constructed. Make sure that proposals enhance rather than detract from the original design.

A legal contract with the contractor obviously needs to be completed. Once again, when dealing with lawyers it is good to have someone who will be part of the team. Although it may not be a bonus for the lawyer financially, it will work very well for you. An old house is not comprised of black and white, but many shades of gray. This grayness leads to many changes in the process, many of which will take place during the day, when neither you nor the lawyer can be present. These are unavoidable matters. The most effective manner of dealing with them is for all parties to keep a log, where all changes are noted, dated and when possible, signed on the same day. These logs are then transferred to the lawyer, so that all records are in one complete log. You really do need somebody who is sympathetic to the principles of preservation to be your legal counsel.

Financially, when embarking on a project of this scale most people have a mortgage with a financial institution. How much more money will you need to complete the restoration project? How much (and this is incredibly important) will the property be worth at the end of the process? Make comparisons, and get some local realtors in who can show you pricing for similar properties in the area. If you have paid $100,000 for the house and you want to spend another $100,000, but houses in the area generally go for only $150,000, you may want to consider this disparity. This may not concern you; you may be willing to spend that extra amount to have what you want. But look at market value, realtors' figures and the willingness of the bank to support your wishes. Although period hardware is totally fabulous, the next buyer who comes along may not give a hoot about it. The bank certainly doesn't care: they are far more interested in marketability and square-footage costs.

I have a rule of thumb when approaching a project. First I measure the exterior walls — for example, if the building is two storeys high, 30 feet wide and 40 feet long, then I end up with 1200 square feet times two storeys, which gives me 2400 square feet. Then I look at what price custom-built homes are being built for in this area — for example, $80 per square foot. At that price the replacement value of this house will theoretically be $192,000, not including the price of the lot. Although this is not an exact figure, it is accurate in bankers' terms, because they will come on board oblivious to the architectural integrity of the building. They are, however,

ABOVE

A great neo-Gothic entranceway.

OPPOSITE

The ultimate in a restored log house, featuring an eclectic mix of period furniture.

Period furnishings always enhance the period room.

Colonial architecture was born of tradition and available materials.

very concerned with square footage and number of rooms, if not with the visual splendor of the living-room baseboards.

Once you've bought the house and all the commotion has died down, take a chair and sit in the house. Look around and take in exactly what you have purchased. The house will tell you how to approach its preservation. Books, architects and designers, friends and family, even your dog, will all give you advice. Be careful about acting impulsively. Go slowly and let the house be your guide. Follow it and you will have an excellent journey.

PHOTO DOCUMENTATION

It is imperative to totally document, photographically, every stage of the preservation process. This includes as-found photos of all exterior walls, roofs and other architectural features, as well as all wall elevations within the house. A log should be kept with the accompanying photographs and dated. Any pertinent changes should be recorded. The landscape is as important to document as the structure itself.

Photographs record the preservation process in a way in which written description, however good, cannot. They can be made quickly and often cost much less than measured drawings, often accomplishing things that drawings can only with considerable labor.

The number of photographs to be taken of a structure will be determined by its complexity, interest and importance. These factors will allow you to estimate what views are necessary for a minimum record (when resources are limited) and for an optimum record (under better circumstances). For purposes of analysis you should divide the study of a building into five parts: exterior general views, exterior details, interior details, and unusual or special features.

The number of interior general photographs will depend on the interior design. One shot, showing most of two walls or an end wall with part of the adjoining two sides, may be sufficient for a single room. However, when opposite walls are to be featured two photographs are required.

Wherever items of special interest or significance — such as decorative arts, historic lighting or heating fixtures, uncommon construction or gardening accessories — are encountered, they should be recorded.

ANALYSIS OF STRUCTURE

Part A

Location: _____

Physical Period: _____

Condition to Period: _____

Social Period: _____

Part B

Structural Foundation System: _____

Exterior

a. Cladding: _____
   clapboard: _____
   board and batten: _____
   shingle: _____
   other: _____

b. Log: _____

c. Deterioration: _____
   insect: _____
   rot: _____
   human abuse: _____
   decay (air pollution): _____
   moisture: _____
   structural defects: _____
   replacement materials: _____
   fenestration/windows: _____
   doors: _____
   sills: _____

d. Roof: _____
   cladding (shingles, tin, etc.): _____
   flashing (chimneys, valleys): _____
   rafter ends: _____
   soffit and fascia: _____
   planking of roof: _____
   eavestrough: _____
   bargeboard: _____
   chimney (materials, pointing, etc.): _____
   hardware: _____

e. Masonry: _____
   stone/brick/stucco: _____
   structural: _____
   pointing: _____
   cleaning: _____
   coatings: _____

f. Chimneys: _____

Interior

a. Structure: _____

b. Walls (plaster, lath): _____

c. Molding (door trim, paneling, baseboard): _____

d. Doors: _____

e. Hardware: _____

f. Plasterwork: _____

g. Paint: _____

h. Stairs: _____

i. Railings: _____

j. Fireplaces: _____

k. Mechanical Systems: _____
   electrical: _____
   plumbing: _____
   heating: _____
   venting systems: _____

Site Analysis

a. Levels: _____

b. Vegetation: _____

c. Drainage: _____

d. Access: _____

e. Fencing: _____

f. Mechanical Requirements: _____

RIGHT
Urban decay often offers opportunities to the would-be preservationist.

BELOW
The White Swan Tavern in Burritts Rapids, Ontario, awaits restoration.

CLOCKWISE FROM TOP LEFT

Surprise! A clapboard house was really a log house.

A diamond in the rough.

A well restored house in New Brunswick, circa 1840.

CHAPTER THREE

Survey and Assessment

Although you may notice obvious repairs and changes that you want to make to your "new old house," you must not let your enthusiasm impair your judgment. There is no point in spending money on paint and detailing until you have first examined the structural integrity of the building. It is usually wise to bring in an expert who is familiar with period architecture. Contractors who are familiar only with modern homes might suggest that you rip your old dream down and start afresh. Consult a restoration specialist.

The structural integrity of a building can be compromised in a variety of ways. The major culprit is moisture. This can be imposed on the building by the conditions of the surrounding soil, thermal upgrading, lack of adequate vapor barriers and/or the effects of the freeze–thaw cycle in Northern climes. The building can also be suffering from overloading, excavations and mechanical vibrations, which, when added to the assault of dampness, prove to be too much for a once-healthy structure. Second to moisture, human abuse is probably the most common cause of deterioration in a building.

Actual physical leaks in the structure, whether in the cladding, the roof, the soffit-and-fascia or the flashing, can cause structural breakdown. The physical damage, as mentioned earlier, can come when areas of the building are expected to perform tasks they were never meant to do. For example, a grand piano in the living room can cause undue stress on a beam that was not meant to carry that weight. Mechanical vibrations from new mechanical systems, furnace and duct work inserted throughout the house can also cause damage. Mechanical upgrades are also culprits where thoughtless plumbers or electricians have introduced new systems by cutting through existing beams and studs. Leaking from the aforementioned plumbing can eventually lead to the arrival of wet and/or dry rot, which in turn leads to structural failure.

It is imperative to do the structural analysis in a "partial" manner. This does not mean that you are not thorough; instead, it means that you analyze small parts of the system at a time. There are two obvious reasons for doing this. First, if you try to do it all at once, the situation can become out of control and you will find yourself overwhelmed by too many details and possibly too much cost. The secondary factor is one of safety. If a large portion of the structure has a major problem, there is a possibility that it could collapse. Obviously you should avoid this, by stabilizing the offending area before further drastic deterioration takes place.

Two areas of concern in exterior deterioration can occur with the build-up of the contour soil over a period of years, whether because of sidewalks where the grade has risen over the original foundation, or just a general build-up of vegetation over the century. These situations can often change the drainage patterns so that rather than draining away from the house, guttering systems may actually be draining into the house and into the foundation. The ultimate failure of the foundation will expose the sill plates and wood cladding in the surrounding area to decay. Obviously the solution to this problem would be to drain and re-grade the entire area around the existing structure, thus allowing all water-drainage systems to run away from it. Care must be taken here to ensure the safety of period plantings and gardens, for their importance within the overall restoration plan must be considered. It may be necessary to take up all plantings in the surrounding area and then to replant after the drainage problem has been corrected.

The use of foreign materials, such as winter salt, can in itself lead to major deterioration of wooden sills and

RIGHT AND OPPOSITE
**Examination and
discovery of wet rot in
an Italianate form
house, from early
19th-century Maine.**

can cause problems where ordinary wear is the only constant. Sprinkling sand instead of salt on icy pathways can prevent any further problems in this area. An added bonus is that the sand can be raked into your lawn and gardens without causing concern.

A foundation is usually made up of a small pad with a wall created on top of it. Occasionally, in earlier buildings, you may find that a pad was not used. However, most buildings of the nineteenth century would have a pad running approximately six to ten inches on either side of the foundation wall. The wood structure would sit on top of the foundation wall. Obviously, when problems occur with the foundation wall they transfer into the wood system itself.

The basement or crawlspace must be continually checked for signs of moisture and lack of ventilation. Because moisture is the main culprit in deterioration, adequate venting and drainage must be provided.

Where there is wet in the basement, such as streams, ponds and other major water build-up, you should install weeping tile. The ideal scenario is to lay weeping tile around the perimeter of the building. This would be done by excavating, parging the foundation and installing weeping tile and drainage tile within the exposed space. While it is excavated you should insulate the foundation, tar over that and then backfill with crushed stone. In some cases, because the surrounding area is built up, it is not possible to excavate the perimeter of the building. Therefore, weeping tile will have to be installed within the actual basement at approximately two to four feet from the existing foundation wall, so as not to undermine it in any way. A trench should be dug approximately one foot deep and weeping tile installed, surrounded by crushed stone. The tile should run the perimeter of the basement to a pit in one corner. This becomes the sump pit, where a sump

A new concrete foundation has been placed under the existing wooden house (in Limington, Maine). It has been capped with stone from the original foundation.

Joists have dropped from their pockets in the main beam, caused by structural failure elsewhere in the building system.

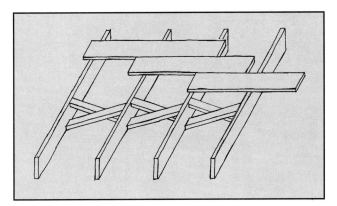

Cross bridging.

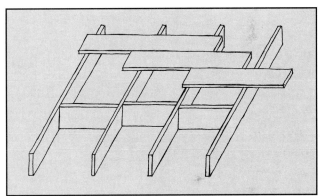

Block bridging.

TOP LEFT

A combination of traditional joinery and contemporary epoxy work has resulted in in-situ joist restoration.

MIDDLE LEFT

New joist hangers and new joist ends have stabilized a major structural problem.

BOTTOM LEFT

An architectural column is restored by removal and replacement of rotted sections.

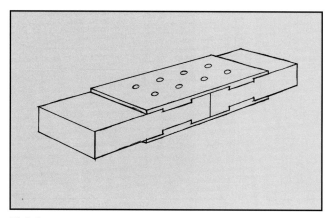

Fishplate.

pump is immersed permanently to drain out the offending water.

In our experience it has always been found useful not only to put some form of tile into the basement, but also to pour a concrete floor where there is an earth floor in existence. This ensures a cool, dry stable area in the basement that can be controlled in terms of humidity and protected from condensation. It has also been our practice to employ fans within the basement area to allow for the movement of air in summer and winter. In summer one has the problem of condensation from the coolness of the exterior soil against the foundation wall, especially if it is not insulated. Even with an insulated perimeter, some coolness permeates the basement and causes condensation below the actual insulated area. In winter the reverse is true: the heat should be moved around to ensure adequate drying throughout. It is often important to add damp-proof courses just below the point at which the beams meet the rubblestone or masonry wall.

Where an actual basement wall or crawlspace has failed totally, it is important to undertake a process

known as "underpinning." This involves shoring the joists within the structure and the remaining perimeter walls in place with a series of jack posts. You then excavate the failed section of walling, pour or set a new foundation (preferably with the same type of foundation or footing that already exists in the rest of the structure), or rebuild a new wall with the same kind of building techniques and materials used in the original. This is not a project to be undertaken by the amateur. It should be professionally executed and documented with photographs and drawings. When dealing with the framework of the structure — the walls, the roof, the interior walls — remember to use compatible or identical building materials when restoring or replacing damaged areas.

A telltale way of examining the exterior damage within the walls of a house is to stand at the corners of the walls and literally eyeball the walls. If there is bulging or indentation, or if it seems like the wall is bowing in or out, there is a very good chance that structural failure is taking place from within, or in fact the roof is pushing down and causing the wall to spring out.

The interior of the house often gives us clues as to what is wrong with the exterior, or at least underneath the shell of the exterior. Doors that seem to close by banging into the floor, sagging floors, door trim that has developed a decided cant — all of these clues indicate settlement or failure within the framework of the house. One very simple way to detect the levelness of the structure is to place a marble in the center of the wooden floor. If it tends to always roll in one direction, then you know that there is a settlement problem. One associate of ours purchased a period house in Virginia. On inspection he noted that the exterior walls had settled more than the interior chimney, leaving an inch ledge where the hearth and floorboards met.

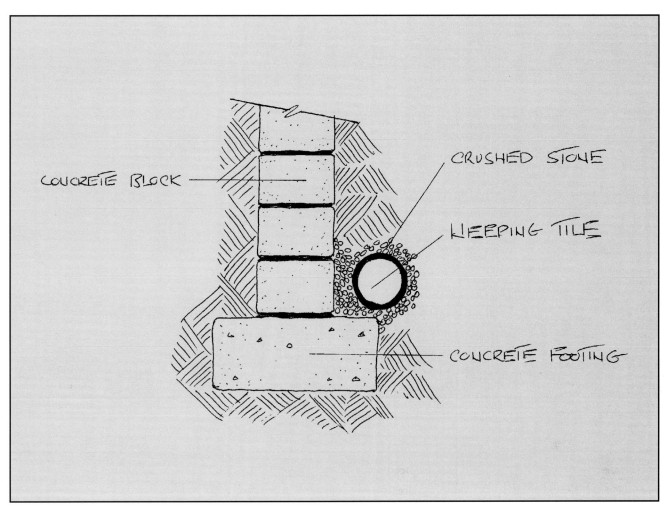

It is important to ensure controlled drainage by placement of weeping tiles.

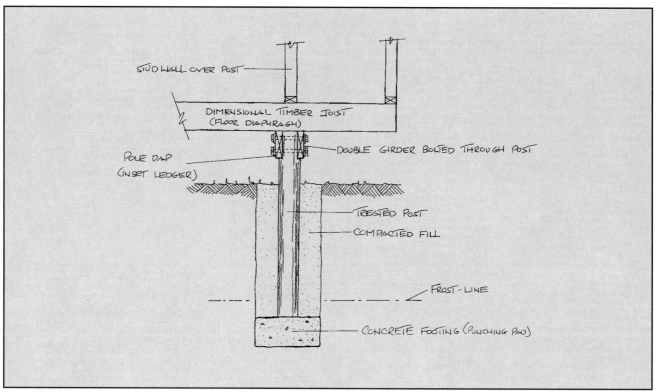

STUD WALL OVER POST

DIMENSIONAL TIMBER JOIST
(FLOOR DIAPHRAGH)

POLE DAP
(INSET LEDGER)

DOUBLE GIRDER BOLTED THROUGH POST

TREATED POST

COMPACTED FILL

FROST-LINE

CONCRETE FOOTING (PUNCHING PAD)

Pole foundation plan.

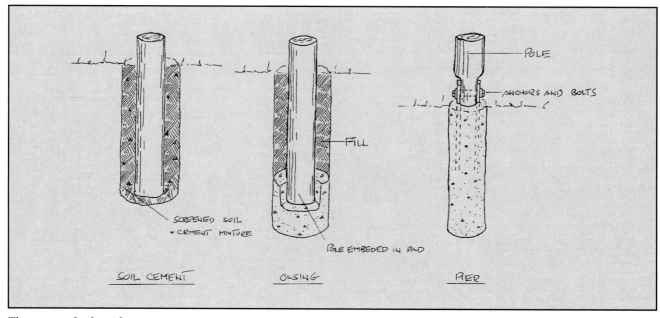

POLE

ANCHORS AND BOLTS

FILL

SCREENED SOIL
+ CEMENT MIXTURE

POLE EMBEDED IN PAD

SOIL CEMENT   CASING   PIER

Three types of pole anchors.

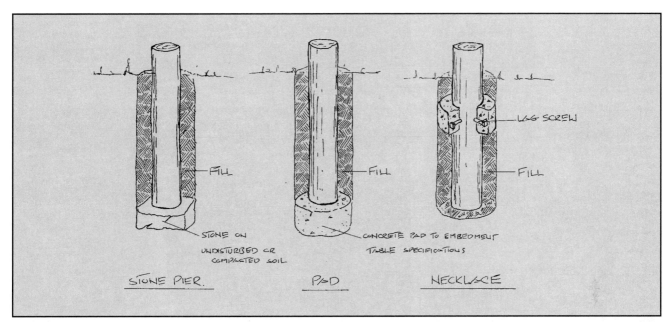

Three types of piers.

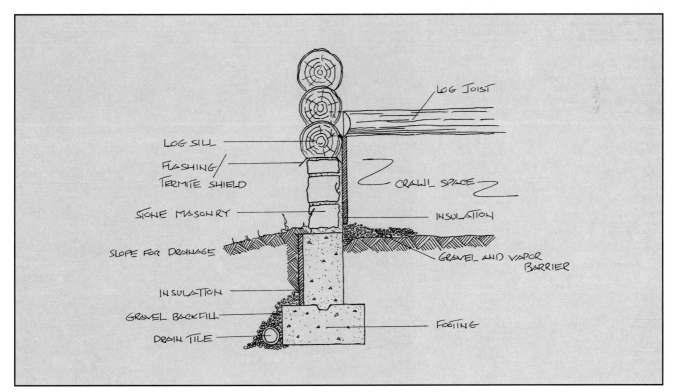

A good foundation ensures a sound building.

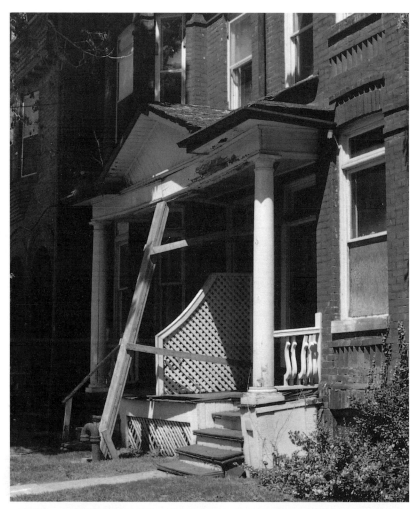

Porch detail from the late nineteenth century. The footings, roof system, column and stairs are all failing, due to lack of maintenance and the ravages of moisture.

Drainage should be well away from the foundation.

Traditional ceiling framing.

Traditional guttering methods can be used as long as they drain properly.

Major structural damage was
evident in the dissembly of this
1840 frame structure.

A series of 19th-century room layouts. Indicating areas of structural deterioration on your floor plans allows a constant reference point.

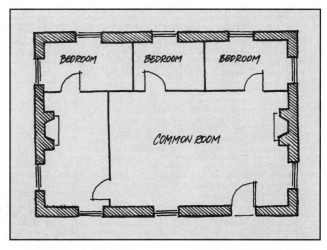

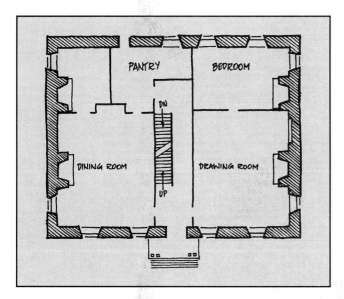

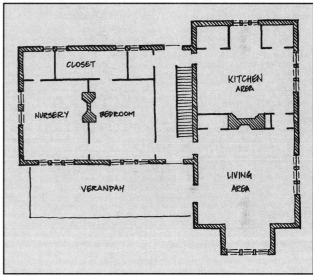

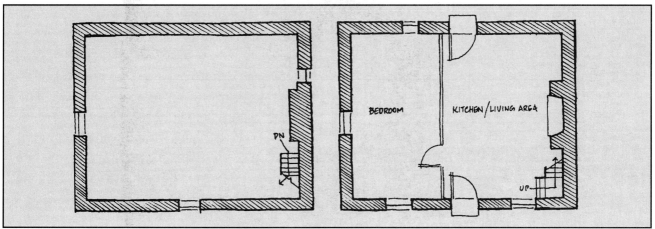

Telltale frass shows potential carpenter-ant infestation.

Remedial procedures may be as simple as replacing jack posts that have rotted off in the basement. Where steel posts, or in fact where new wooden posts are employed and jacking is to occur, it is imperative that the jacking process take place slowly, over a period of weeks, so as not to undo the rest of the settlement that has taken place over a given amount of years. Often one will find that over a month one can jack floors back into level balance, so that the doors no longer need trimming or the trim adjusting, because they are in fact returning to their original configuration.

Once again, ask yourself why you bought an old house. Some degree of sagging or swaying, as long as it doesn't indicate structural failure, is not really a problem as far as we are concerned. Sometimes, in fact, undersized joints were used in the original construction of the house, and modern lifestyles are merely requiring a system to perform in a way that was never intended. Whenever "beefing up" such systems, a certain degree of give and take must occur with the wooden house. What is rigid will tend to break; what is given flexibility will last a long time.

Replacing or repairing areas of timber that have failed, and addressing the conditions that lead to that failure, are of paramount importance. However, make absolutely certain that you have also eradicated the agent of destruction. Fungi and insects are major culprits in deterioration. Whenever there is evidence of fungal and/or insect deterioration, look for the cause. Four main elements are necessary for fungal and insect rotting to occur. Moisture is always the number-one culprit. A house should be able to shed water in all of its forms — liquid, vapor and ice. Air must also be present; these creatures can't flourish in a vacuum. They must also have a livable temperature. Finally, these attackers need a food

Structural failure, due to wet rot and fungal infestation.

Carpenter-ant infestation, from the same house.

source. Theoretically, if you remove these problems, you will also remove the culprits they attract.

When a tree is cut down, deterioration begins. Fungi are parasitical and live by feeding on organic matter. Your house is partially made up of organic matter. *Moruvious lachrimans,* nicknamed "dry rot," is a devastating fungus that requires a supply of moisture (20 percent), a suitable temperature (65 degrees Fahrenheit), a food supply and, of course, the spore of the fungus itself. The spore lands on an appropriate area of timber and in a stiff, stuffy atmosphere throws out whole strands, known as hypha. The hypha transforms rapidly into a cotton-like structure known as mycelium, which is at first white, but then turns yellow with purple spots on it. It then develops strands, called rhizomorphs, which convey moisture from the decomposing wood to the sound timber. When it is well established, the fungus will produce a sporophore, or flower, which becomes a fruiting body carrying millions of spores or seeds. A sporophore may give out two to five million spores per square foot, and they are carried everywhere in a fine red dust that will germinate and start afresh. Although this fungus likes to eat fresh wood, it will go anywhere in your house — along and through joists, and through walls, damp newspapers and books. Symptoms are a musty smell, fleshy mycelium or fruiting bodies, bulging of joinery where the timber has been attacked and is actually bursting out, and a hollow or dead sound in the material, with deep cracks across the grain.

Wherever dry rot is found in a building, it is imperative to remove all existing material that comes in contact with it. Wherever the material cannot be removed, a fungicide must coat the offending wood. It is imperative that this be saturated; holes must be drilled and injected in all forms or planes of the wood. All infected pieces that have been removed should be burned some distance away from the site. The biggest enemy of dry rot is air and the movement of it. If you can provide ventilation, you will check the growth of dry rot.

Other minor fungi, sometimes called wet rot, are not quite as virulent as dry rot. Cellar fungus, or *corneophorous erabella,* is commonly found in the damp, dark areas of the basement. It cannot live on timber with a moisture content of less than 25 percent. It has fine, dark brown or blackish strands in a green, leathery, lumpy fruiting body. A thin shell of sound wood is left on the surface of the timber, while along the inside it's eaten away. Deep cracks along the grain are telltale signs of this. Usually, by cutting out the offending area, burning all infected timber and, of course, removing the inviting conditions, you will put an end to wet rot.

However, many experts still recommend treating wood with a fungicide as a precaution.

Fungicides should be applied by using a brush, by injecting or by spraying under low pressure. Whenever new materials are added to replace old or infected materials, it is imperative that they be saturated, as well, with the fungicide or insecticide.

The three basic types of wood preservant are: tar-oil preservants, waterborne salt preservants and organic solvents. Organic solvents are the most popular for the treatment of in situ timber. The fungicides incorporated in these preservatives are either pentachlorophenol, copper or zinc naphthalene, and chlorinated naphthalene. It is imperative to remember that these chemicals are toxic to humans and must be used with great caution.

With fungi, you have growths that appear somewhat stationary, even though you may notice their increasing proportions on a daily basis. When insects decide to take up residence in your home, thriving and feasting on the tasty wood materials that are present, you may feel like the victim of an undesirable houseguest. An invasion of carpenter ants, marching through your home, oblivious to your shrieks and stomps of protest, can prove quite disconcerting. Know that they mean business. We cannot possibly deal with every kind of insect that attacks wood. For the purposes of this book, we will look at the four main insects found in wood in North America.

The death watch beetle has a life cycle of three to ten years, and so you may only find the evidence of its work and not the beetle itself. It is attracted to damp, warm timber, usually preferring hardwood or even old hardened timber. Sometimes it will be concentrated inside damp walling, and can often be discovered in combination with a fungal attack. At night you can

These photos show the examination and restoration of a balloon-framed house with front elevation, from Eastern Ontario.

actually hear the death watch beetle chipping away as it eats the wood. The rapping sound is a mating call.

The furniture beetle enjoys both softwood and hardwood, and once again moist, wet or damaged timber is its first choice. As the name suggests, this beetle will often be brought into the house with a prized piece of antique furniture. One dear friend was sitting in a comfortable parlor chair, carrying on a delightful conversation, when he suddenly found himself on the floor. One of the legs of this charming piece of furniture had finally crumbled away, victim to the aforementioned beetle.

There is often confusion when trying to distinguish termites from carpenter ants. Termites are not ants, even though at first glance you may have trouble seeing any difference. Subterranean termites actually live in the soil, where they live off the moist earth. Without this moisture they will die. Their interest in your wood is as a food source. They are usually found in the Pacific Coastal regions of North America. The dry wood termite, on the other hand, lives in dry wood and may attack buildings as well as furniture. It is found on the Pacific Coast and in Southern Ontario. Termites can eat the woody structure of a house from within, often leaving a painted surface undamaged.

Carpenter ants, which are much larger than termites or common ants, prefer wood that has been softened by decay or moisture. There you will find cleaned-out tunnels, which serve as the ants' nests. They do not eat the wood, as do termites, but prefer sweeter food sources and organic decay. Examine the soft wood around plumbing leaks, clogged gutters or similar spots. The queen lives in the main nest, often found in the space behind drywall, insulation, etc. Carpenter ants can often be heard at night. One acquaintance asked for a consultation after hearing weird sounds in his wall each

night. Sure enough, it was a colony of industrious carpenter ants, tunneling through a portion of one of his structural beams, leaving the telltale piles of frass (a fine, powdery sawdust residue from the tunnels) behind.

To prevent attacks of fungi or insects, deal with moisture problems, provide adequate ventilation and keep all areas clean. Storing firewood well away from the house, and trimming bushes and trees so that their branches do not provide a bridge to your home, are proactive moves. Sometimes the queen, or a reproductive member of the colony, will fly through an unscreened window and begin her work in the first suitable place she can find.

While a general discussion of rot and fungicides is imperative to the layperson, and to the restoration process overall, it is a subject best left to the professionals. Intervention by the unschooled can lead to inadequate solutions, and more importantly to major physical harm for humans, beast and vegetation. Check local legislation before embarking on any attempt to tackle the problem.

Unfortunately, often the only solution that will be offered in dealing with these pests involves the use of highly toxic substances. These chemicals can cause longterm health problems, and specially made protective gear must be worn when they are being applied. Vacate the premises for at least 48 hours, removing all food and food utensils. Upon your return clean all areas with which small children and animals may come in contact.

There are a number of folk remedies that are supposed to chase away these unwanted guests. In fact, cucumber slices and leaves of basil have not been known, in our experience, to have any effect at all on the carpenter ant. However, growing mint around doorways does seem to deter the common black kitchen ant from entering our household.

ABOVE LEFT

Making sure that details are well maintained is essential.

ABOVE RIGHT

The elements are all there, but in obvious need of restoration.

LEFT

A new roof system, applied to a 19th-century log house.

RIGHT AND BELOW
Often architectural fragments can be used to replace a whole section. Note the wheel window.

Plaster molding and trim in poor condition, but restorable.

ABOVE
Repair, rather than replacement, is the essence of architectural preservation.

CHAPTER FOUR

Exteriors

A house is made up of a number of elements: the exterior walls, the roof system, the floors, the interior trim, the windows and doors. All of these components are subject to deterioration.

The roof or "hat" of the house is made up of a number of components. Structurally it sits on the main body of the house and is made up of trusses, rafters or a combination of both. These are constructed in a particular manner that will keep the roof in place. On top of the trusses or rafters sit the sheathing and on top of this you could find some form of cladding — straw, slate, or in the case of this text, wood. The wood could be rough planks laid across each other. On top of these planks you might find heavy-wood split shingle, or, in the later nineteenth century, you might have found sawn shingle. Wood would have to be cut and shaped to accommodate the chimney openings and, in later times, plumbing stacks or even added architectural elements such as dormers. Surrounding the roof, like a brim on the edge of a hat, is the soffit-and-fascia and cornice combination. This in turn will also hold the eavestroughing, which diverts rainwater or melting snow away from the structure, so that it doesn't drip down the facade or into the foundation. In its simplistic form, the eavestrough is merely a device that sheds water. In its more refined architectural form it can also be the decorative trim surrounding the hat.

When the hat we are wearing becomes wet and worn, we repair or replace it. We should do no less for the house. Shingles wear out, flashing in the valleys around the dormers wears out, flashing around chimneys and stacks wears out. Wherever possible, re-roofing takes place. Usually the actual sheathing of the roof is still in good condition, but some planks may need to be replaced, and some rafters may need drastic removal. If the roof has been left in poor condition for a long time, there may be serious deterioration taking place in the actual rafter system. Generally speaking, if the roof has been well maintained, the problems in the house will be minor.

Because of the cost of replacing a roof, original decorative details often get lost, knocked off or even removed. This is often true in Victorian-style homes, the majority of which scatter throughout the Northeastern U.S.A. and Eastern Canada. Many a decorative peak or gable of ornate gingerbread has been sawn off so that a new roof could be easily installed. It is imperative in preservation to deal sensitively with the character of the exterior building. This involves carefully applying flashing to such elements as the peaks on gables, or the area where the eavestrough marries into the soffit-and-fascia, rather than ripping away the charm of those decorative elements. Work with them and with a design that will be in harmony with the structure.

Although we have mentioned the moisture from above (rainstorms and snow), we must also deal with a more insidious problem — moisture from within. Warm air rises and carries moisture with it. It is very important to have the roof system well ventilated, and this ventilation should carry through right into the soffit-and-fascia. There must be a movement of air throughout the roof system. Older buildings, because of their lack of insulation, inherently allowed for movement of air. Over the past 30 years our zealousness to seal everything up has lead to greater problems than any coolness experienced from lack of insulation. Poorly installed vapor barriers lead to a build-up of condensation in the attic space.

OPPOSITE

A fine Georgian entrance.

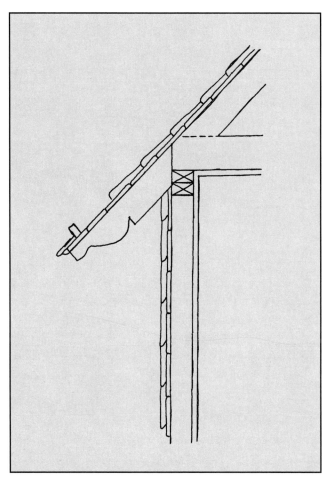

Open cornice.

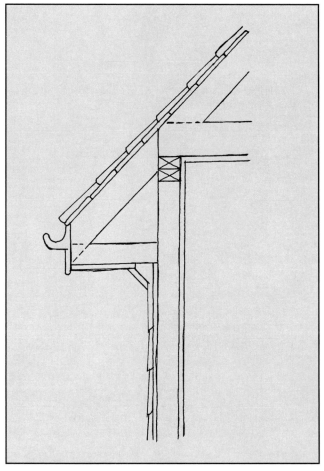

Box cornice.

Cornice detail showing massive moisture problems, in spite of the period vents.

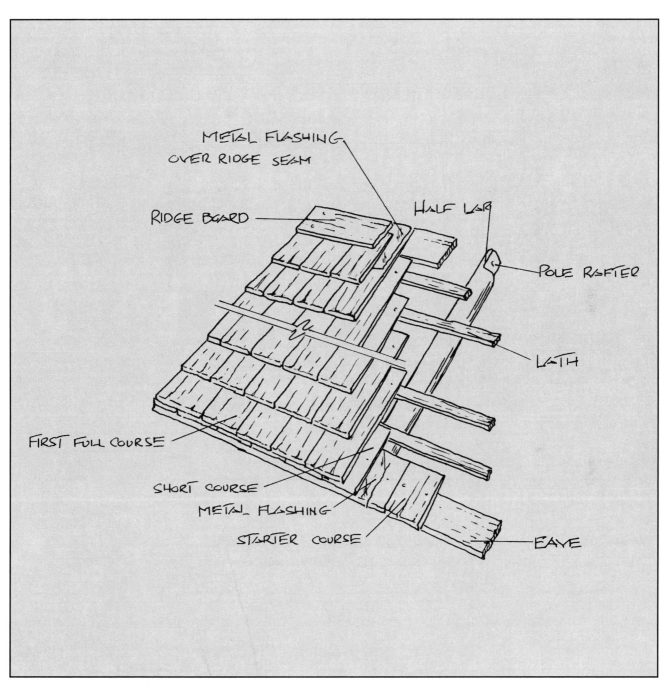

A well vented roof system is imperative.

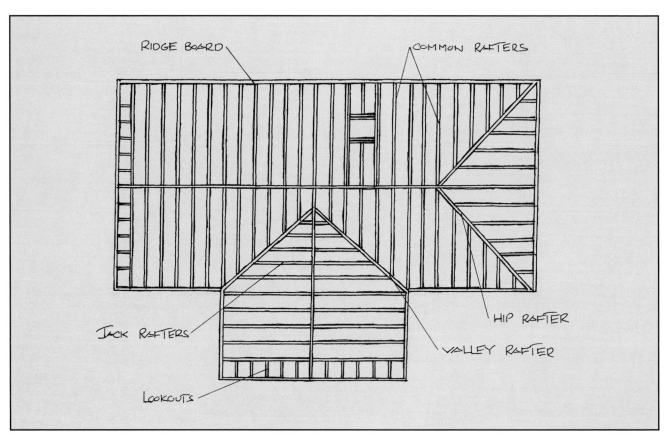

ABOVE

Various rafter type.

RIGHT

Collar beam roof.

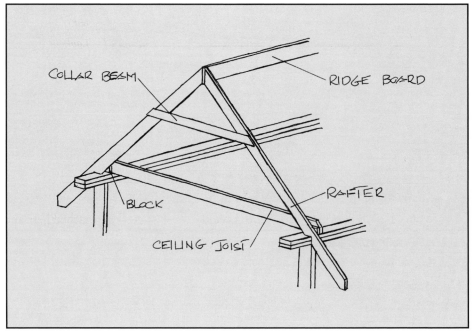

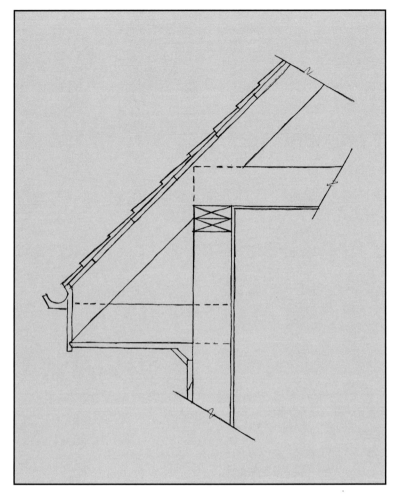

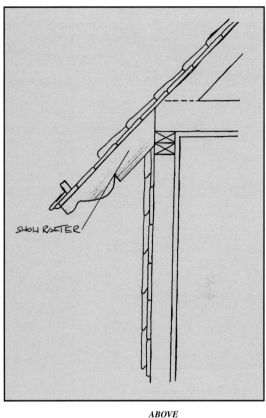

ABOVE
Show rafter.

LEFT
Lookout.

This means that moisture becomes trapped in the roof system. What often occurs is that the area between the rafters is framed and insulated. Because of a contractor or do-it-yourselfer's lack of familiarity with period construction, improper vapor barriers are installed. These then become blocked off, causing an end to air movement within these spaces. As the freeze–thaw cycle occurs, condensation builds up in the area, which in turn leads to wet rot, which in turn leads to material breakdown and failure of rafters and systems within the roof structure. This can also occur where rafter ends extend beyond the exterior walls. The soffit-and-fascia will be attached here and can eventually fall to the ground because the wood to which they were attached has rotted away. Rather than replacing the entire system, it is often more expedient just to cover the damaged area with some lesser architectural treatment. As a matter of the house's general maintenance program, eavestrough

Rafters with birdsmouth cuts.

False rafter.

Rafter tail.

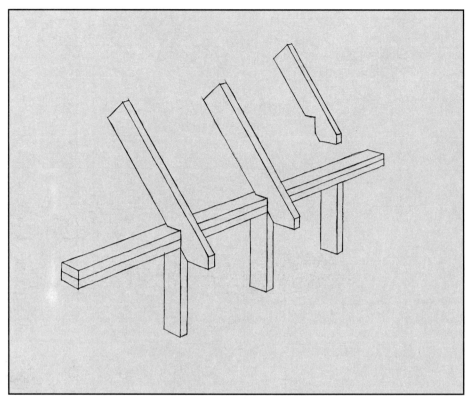

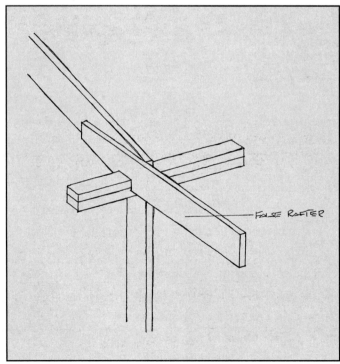

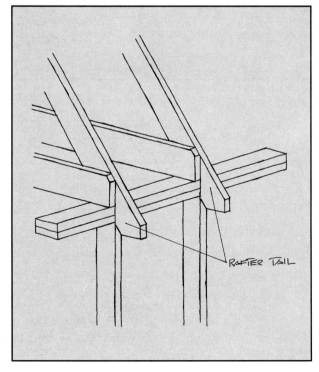

An outstanding timber frame Saltbox house, late 18th century.

*The Industrial Revolution still offered an artistic scope to the
builder/designer. Note the outstanding porch detailing.*

*Function and layout often dictated the basic design of the period
homestead.*

Artist Gary Nichol's homestead in the upper Ottawa Valley has inspired a series of paintings.

A diamond in the rough. Built in 1840, clad in board and batten in the late 19th century, this large log house awaits restoration.

Interior joinery is splendidly simple in this mid-19th-century house.

ABOVE AND BELOW **Built-in cupboards were the exception rather than the rule.**

A superb example of the itinerant painter's art.

Exuberant joinery in a built-in armoir (Quebec mid-18th century).

Builders would frequently bring their often naive brilliance to a project. Note the outstanding mid-19th-century newel post.

Period furnishings complement period houses.

A beautiful marriage between mantelpiece and a period chest of drawers.

And so to sleep....

Sill repair and maintenance is an ongoing preservation concern.

and downspout should be cleaned out at least twice a year (spring and fall). This allows rain and melting ice or snow an easy exit from the structure.

The other serious problem that can occur in eave–roof deterioration happens once again because of improper venting. It is due to the freeze–thaw cycle that takes place in the Northern U.S.A. and Canada during the winter months, when the temperature fluctuates between warm and cool. Ice builds up within the eavestrough and the external warming temperature, combined with the heat, escapes from an inadequately vented soffit-and-fascia. This causes ice to build up and creep under the shingles, subsequently melting and leaking through the house.

Our original impression of a house, which can stay with us long after we've driven by, is gleaned by that first glance of the external facade. Before we even notice the condition of the roof, our eyes will be draw to the exterior walls. In those external walls are two architectural elements of both practical usage and visual delight. They are the windows and the doors. The front door, without doubt, is the focal point of the whole house. It focuses the eye and welcomes the visitor. In the past it was the statement by which the outside world knew the inhabitant's position in life.

The door itself, the framework and the ornamentation around that doorway, are not only a statement of the inhabitant's lifestyle but a triumph of the builder's craft. The front door welcomes us into the life of the owner and family. It can be welcoming or not. Folk legends and superstitions abound around the potency of the front door and its threshold. One favorite custom of today can be traced back to these times: a timber-framed house would have a large sill, and a groom would carry his new bride over the threshold because it was believed that if she tripped bad luck

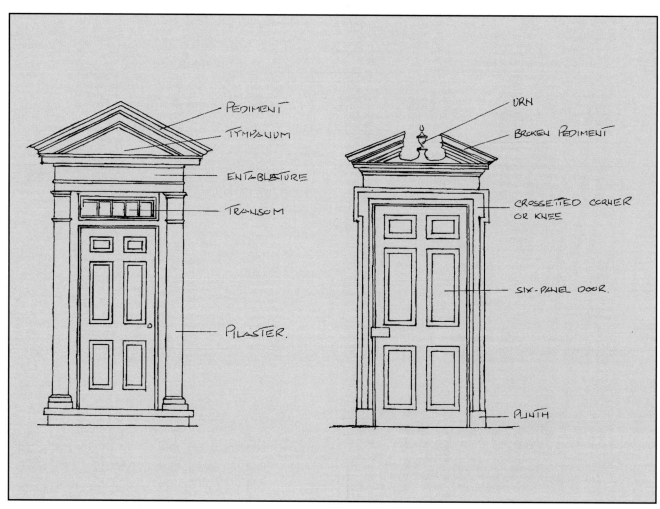

ABOVE AND OPPOSITE

Door and entranceway details.

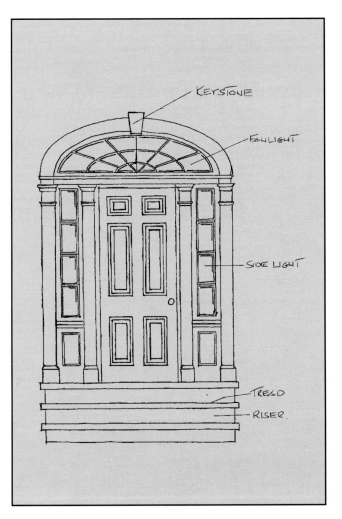

KEYSTONE

FANLIGHT

SIDE LIGHT

TREAD

RISER

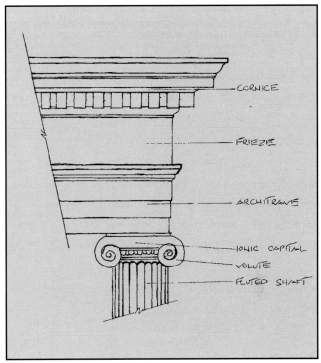

CORNICE

FRIEZE

ARCHITRAVE

IONIC CAPITAL

VOLUTE

FLUTED SHAFT

would follow them throughout their life. By avoiding that possibility, they could be assured that they were embarking on a happy life together.

A blanket of woven branches perhaps made up the most basic form of door. The earliest wooden doors were merely rudimentary groupings of planks fastened together, one side running horizontally, the other side vertically. These could be held together by some type of fastening — wooden pins, dowels, even animal hide. As these board doors evolved, hinges and rudimentary hardware were employed. The nails used were made from a soft, handmade metal, and would be driven through the wood and then bent over to hold the planks together — a process known as clinching. It is interesting to note that

in some larger houses that have evolved over time, board doors may still be used for one of the lesser outbuildings, or as the entrance to the back summer kitchen.

Although French and Spanish settlements employed panel doors from the 1600s, one does not find panels in English North America until the early 1700s.

The restoration of the door and the door surround is probably one of the most important aspects of the preservation of the character and style of the property. It will set the tone and provide the dominant mood for the entire project. Because it is a working element of architecture, the door is subject to a large amount of use and misuse. Before you start on an adventure to restore the door, inspect and record all details: the hardware, the

Cornice restoration.

hinging, the sills, the sidelights, the fanlight above, the paneling — every detail. The door itself will actually be hung within a framework, and the entire framework will have been framed into the body or wall of the house. If one is lucky enough to be able to expose the entire framework with the door hung intact, one can lift out — almost like a jigsaw puzzle — the entire door assembly, similar to how one may place a new window or door unit today.

Many items in the period structure were made in components, and this applies as much to a doorframe and door as to other sections. One should try to follow the original when restoring the door and frame. Often the sill will be in poor condition, but if it is mortice-and-tenoned it is possible to disassemble it and make a new sill with the same dimensions and configurations of the original. Woodwork surrounding the door often becomes worn over time, and elements of trim may be missing.

Replace as accurately as possible with similar types of trim and detailing. The door itself may become scratched or shrunk or experience cracking for a number of reasons: misuse, constant opening and closing or ongoing effects of inclement weather. Wherever possible, restore rather than replace. If the old door is in extremely poor condition, have a new door constructed exactly as the old one. If it is not possible to disassemble the original door by drilling out its pins and reassembling the original components, replace the items that are too severely damaged to restore.

Too often one finds that after care and attention has been applied to the restoration of a house and its woodwork, the owner will thoughtlessly employ contemporary hardware, negating the preservation process. Wherever possible, use the original hardware or at least accurate reproduction hardware. Adapt such contemporary systems as adjacent security requirements.

READING MOISTURE CONTENT

A moisture meter is an instrument for recording the amount of moisture within a given wood surface. Today a large amount of credence is given to what the moisture meter reads, especially in the wood used for sash, door and trim construction. Remember that early pioneers (and their houses) survived without moisture meters. I have not dwelt on this subject in any great detail in this text. The small chart below will show variable moisture content and requirements.

Recommended Inside Humidity for Varying Outside Temperatures

Outside air temperature (°C)	Recommended inside humidity at 20°C (68°F)
-30 or below	15%
-30 to -24	20%
-24 to -18	25%
-18 to -12	35%
-12 and above	40%

Source: Taken from *Keeping the Heat In*. Energy, Mines and Resources Canada, 1976.

The members of a panel door.

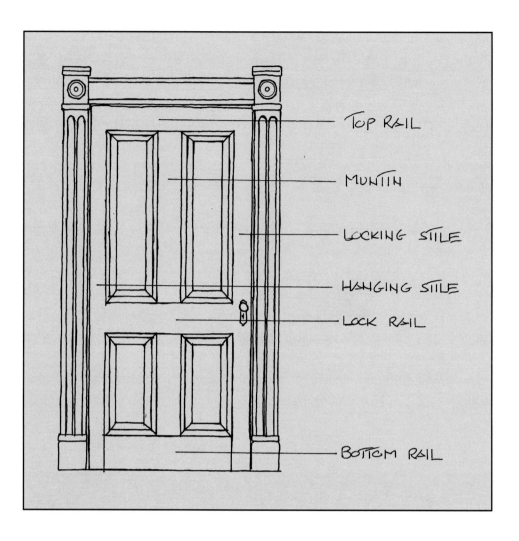

TOP RAIL

MUNTIN

LOCKING STILE

HANGING STILE

LOCK RAIL

BOTTOM RAIL

This can be as simple as deadbolts painted out, or actual bolt systems employed within the interior of the door.

Surrounding sash and sidelights should be restored as per the original. Often, due to today's heating requirements, storm sashes need to be employed, especially where there is a transom light and sidelights. It is often easy to duplicate the original sash and add it as a winter addition to the existing unit. Extreme care must be taken not to disturb or damage architectural elements from the original unit.

Wherever possible, as with anything in an old house, repairing the original is better than replacing it. If you do this, there are some useful products designed specifically for wood repair, mostly for doors, windows and moldings.

The same practice applies to the use of screen doors in summer. Try to add them onto the existing framework rather than replace an entire unit. It is best to work a similar system into a doorframe and employ a new storm or a new screen door. Exterior doors should be checked

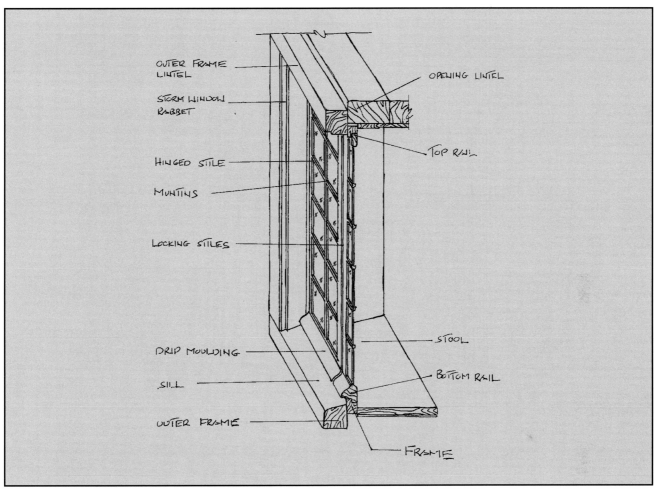

Cross-section of a casement window.

THERMAL VALUE® OF DIFFERENT TYPES OF GLAZING

Single glazing	0.88 to 1.04	Canadian standards for new buildings (R 1.70 corresponds to double glazing with at least a $1/4$ of an inch air space. R 2.55 corresponds to triple glazing: sealed double glass and storm window or sealed triple glass)
Double glazing	1.04 to 2.00	
Window with a storm-window	1.56 to 2.08	
Triple glazing (2+1 window-panes)*	1.85 to 3.17	
Triple glazing (sealed panes)	1.31 to 3.03	

The Canadian standards value: **1.70 to 3.03 (depends on the region considered)**

* In general, triple glazing (sealed) is not installed on old windows; the required work costs proportionally more than the energy saving over double windows.

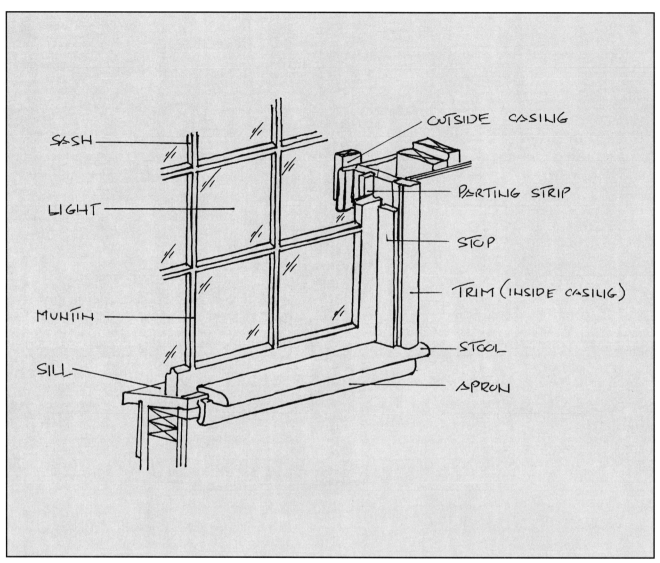

SASH

LIGHT

MUNTIN

SILL

OUTSIDE CASING

PARTING STRIP

STOP

TRIM (INSIDE CASING)

STOOL

APRON

The geography of a double-hung window.

every six months for shrinking, warping, damage or any type of deterioration. Ensure that the bottom of the door is painted. This is one of the highest maintenance areas of the house.

The porch is one of the architectural features of the period wooden house which, again, is practical as well as aesthetic. The front porch was the place, in summer, where folks would gather and socialize and enjoy the warm summer breezes. It was an area of protection from the hot summer sun and from the immediate ferocity of a winter storm. It added an element of protection to the front door and its surround, as well as an imposing architectural element to the structure and style of the house. One may find two-storey porches, sweeping front

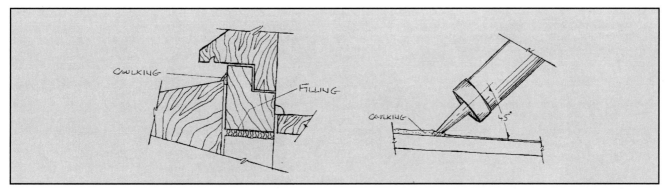

Filling and caulking a sill.   *Caulking with a gun.*

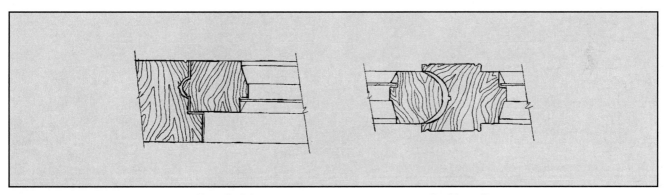

Hinged stile.   *Locking stile.*

PRINCIPAL CAULKING PRODUCTIONS AND THEIR CHARACTERISTICS

Durability	Can be painted?	Use
1. Silicone 20 years +	No	General
2. Polyurethane 20 years +	Yes	General
3. Rubber Butyl 16 years	Yes	Masonry and metal
4. Latex 5 years if painted	Yes	Not recommended for highly exposed locations. Better suited for the interior.

ABOVE LEFT
Animal infestation in the cornice.

ABOVE RIGHT
Adequate guttering is essential to prevent deterioration around the roof.

RIGHT
A board-and-batten gable, roofed in traditional wood shingles. Note the metal valley and new storm-window unit.

porches that surround two sides of the home, and simple entranceways. Rear porches, often referred to as lean-to's, had more rudimentary uses: wood storage, butchering of animals, storage of herbs, cleaning, washing, etc. Whereas today the garage gets filled with all of our trappings and bits, in the nineteenth century the back porch or summer kitchen would serve those purposes.

Porches are often made up of posts, rafters, headers, a cladding and some type of shingle covering. There is a wooden deck, with wooden trelliswork underneath it, which allows air movement. Often the ornamentation style of the house is carried right through to the porch. Porches suffer from the same problems as the rest of the wooden structure. Often foundations are inadequate or have failed over time. In terms of the roof, flashing and shingle cladding may have failed and may need to be replaced.

For structural repair or exterior porch work and fence work, there is a wise tendency these days to use pressure-treated lumber, whether treated with creosote or with copper. It is imperative to be very careful when using these products. For cutting, for handling, for your clothes, make sure all safety precautions are undertaken. These items are extremely toxic.

The window is the eye of the house and can be one of the most visually appealing elements of the structure, but it requires a fair amount of maintenance. Initially, the window was a "win-door" or a "wind-eye," and

TOP LEFT

Interior shutters.

BOTTOM LEFT

A 12-over-12 sash in an 18th-century clapboard house. Note the Indian shutters.

served the purpose of letting light into the interior of the house. Oil paper was used as the first window pane; however, in the early 1600s glassblowers were listed in the record of the early settlers in the Jamestown Settlement. Most glass came from Europe throughout the 1600s. By the mid 1700s it was relatively available throughout the New World, and by the early to mid 1800s there were glassworks throughout North America.

Windows are not just a visual ornament on the facade of the building, they are an element that brings light into our lives. They are designed as a decorative feature that sets a harmony to the overall structure. Therefore, they must be treated in a reverential manner. Not only do they provide the house and its inhabitants with light, but they also provide air for the building to breathe. When dealing with a house that has existed successfully for a hundred years, we must be wary of introducing technology that dramatically alters conditions within that framework. The contemporary overconcern regarding heat loss through windows in period houses must be seriously questioned. If the original unit is replaced with a modern one, one must be aware of the excessive moisture build-up and the inherent condensation problems brought on by inadequate vapor barriers. These may affect cost-efficiency even more than the longterm costs of simply heating the house.

Wherever possible, use the existing window. If repairing or restoring the window isn't possible, then find a suitable alternative. Heat escapes mostly through the roof and through other openings in the building. If the

Blistering and popping of the cladding, indicating inadequate moisture venting from within.

OPPOSITE

A porch and door combination, awaiting restoration.

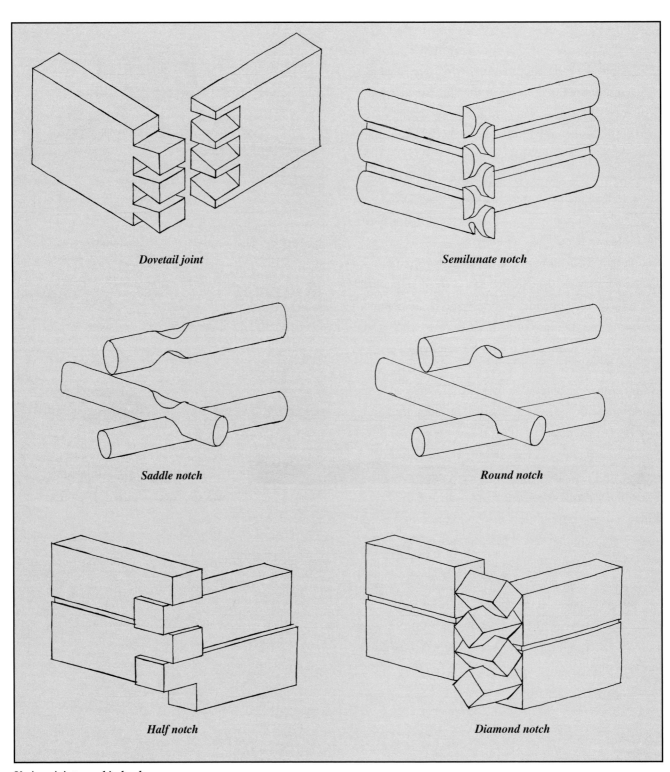

Dovetail joint

Semilunate notch

Saddle notch

Round notch

Half notch

Diamond notch

Various joints used in log houses.

Barge, board and peak detail.

windows are in good condition and have a storm unit, it is preferable to use the existing or restored sash. The window should function in the manner to which it was originally designed. Hardware should be original, or like hardware should be employed. If one is replacing muntins or mullion in the window, it is very important to make sure that they are in the same dimension and profile as the original. Because there is a tendency today to glamorize past fashions, inappropriate, overly elaborate mullions are often employed, distorting not only the window itself, but the entire facade.

Before glass came into common use, our ancestors employed a solid wooden board or panel, which slid back and forth from side to side. The technical term for this type of device was the "draw shutter." We often hear it referred to as the "Indian shutter" — it supposedly offered protection from both inclement weather and Native attacks. William N. Banks noted in the magazine *Antiques* that

> *[t]here is considerable variety in the moldings of the window and doorframes, and only the most ambitious houses boast the nicety of a cornice. Several have windows with inside shutters of the sliding type.*

As mentioned earlier, glass use in North America dates back to the mid 1600s. The Buffin house in Salem, Massachusetts, built between 1642 and 1661, offered at least one casement window with a set of 25 panes, with a row of half-panes tucked in at the bottom to fill it out.

Keeping the Weather Out

The actual body of the house, or framework, is the system to which the exterior cladding is applied. It also protects the interior from the elements. The framework holds the floors in place and supports the roof; it is the system to which the exterior doors and windows, soffit and fascia, and roof system are all tied together. The exterior framework is clad or covered with a sheathing, comprised of planking, which is nailed over it. The sheathing does not always occur. Sometimes the exterior cladding is put directly onto the framework. But in Eastern Canada and the North Eastern United States, because of the inclement weather, there is nearly always a thickness of sheathing applied. Over this, different types of cladding may be applied. These are commonly clapboard (horizontal planking), board and batten (vertical planking) shingles, and decorative planking (which can be vertical or horizontal). Decorative planking was sometimes cut to resemble stone, or some other folk variation. That was the exception rather than the rule and for the most part was used to create an illusion in terms of presentation of being something it was not. We do not refer to this planking as clapboard, but instead we say that it is cut to look like stone because quite honestly stone is more fashionable than clapboard in a given place. These components can also be used in combination. Until the mid-19th century, often cladding would be used in a singular fashion, i.e., you would have a clapboard house or shingled house. As the mass production of wooden components became more readily available through the industrial revolution, combinations occurred. This is shown in extreme in the stick style of

houses. The stick style was born of the building manuals of the mid-19th century. Andrew Jackson Downing was the author of one such book. These were pattern books, and the stick style was really an ornamental expression, rather than an architectural statement. Here, different visual elements and styles of surface treatment, from cross hatching to board and batten, to clapboard to shingle, were all employed in a surface decoration. This style was most popular during the 1860–1870 period, where it evolved into the Queen Anne style, which had a much greater influence throughout the North Eastern U.S. and to some extent in Eastern Canada. The actual term comes from the fact that the horizontal and vertical diagonal boards surrounding the shingle and other cladding were called stick work.

Clapboard is nailed directly onto the framework or sheathing, starting at the base and working upwards. The plank above will overlap the plank below. This works its way up to where the eaves begin, obviously going around windows and doorways, and it is often framed with a cornerboard. The cornerboards are set in place before the clapboard is begun to finish the ends and give a clean and finished appearance to the structure. Clapboard is extremely long lasting. We have examples today in the late 20th century of boarding that was applied in the late 1700s. Always keep in mind that if wood is maintained and kept from moisture, even in exteriors, it is long lasting. European examples date from the 1500s. Wherever damage to clapboard has occurred, it can be repaired. Sections can be cut out and fileted in with new pieces. See photo on page 101.

Board and batten is another form of exterior cladding. It came into popular usage in the mid-19th century with the publication of building manuals and the advent of the Industrial Revolution. Whereas clapboard runs horizontally, board and batten runs vertically. One example is two 12-inch planks butted together with a decorative batten overlapping the joint. These would run from the water table board up to where the cornice meets the roof. This decorative cottage style was born of the romantic Gothic. It was thought to be not only uplifting in form but also proved to be practical. It is extremely weatherproof because every joint is covered with a batten. Preservation is once again easy to deal with. If damage occurs in a section one need only replace that specific area. Whole sections do not need to be removed. In a balloon frame structure because the boards and battens run vertically, some cross bracing must be attached within the framework if sections are going to be replaced. Horizontal cladding, however, can be nailed directly to the vertical. This isn't so much a problem if there is a sheathing underneath the whole structure. Then it's just a matter of nailing directly onto it.

The use of wood shingles and wood shakes are common from the mid 1600s as a surface cladding. They were used on walls and roofs, primarily throughout the Eastern seaboard, and were an effective and reasonable way to weatherproof the sheathing on the framework. It is easy to distinguish the difference between a shake and shingle. The shake is cut by hand from a block of wood using a froe. Shingles are machine cut from a saw and can be regular or shaped in a decorative fashion. Once again, replacement of damaged shingles is relatively simple, as only the damaged areas need to be addressed.

Alternatives to wood cladding (e.g., vinyl or aluminum siding), although heralded in this age as long wearing with low maintenance, do have their own problems. Over a period of time aluminum will fade, chip, and become susceptible to denting, which detracts from the general appearance of the period house. Because of the nature of the material there is also a

tendency for excessive moisture buildup, which leads to deterioration within the framework of the building. When using wood, it is relatively easy to see any problems that may occur. These artificial materials mask, rather than gel with, the ongoing evolution of the period building. We suggest that you avoid them at any cost.

Log Houses

As mentioned earlier, log houses are a rudimentary form of timber frame houses, made of timbers that are square, round and sawn. Like a jigsaw puzzle, they connect — a stack of logs piled on top of each other and joined at the corners. Log houses, the epitome of the romance of frontier living, were in fact initially a primary shelter. Settlers stacked the logs and added a shed-type of roof, and then a door at one end, sometimes with no window. This was a rudimentary place to get through the winter and on to the next year. At times the roofs consisted of bark or plank roofs covered in sod or branches; anything that was available to keep the elements out.

Actual log houses would be made by felling large trees, cutting and squaring the corners and then placing them on top of each other to build a rectangular spiral. For example, in the classic one-and-a-half-storey log house, a foundation would be laid, the first logs would be placed, and the structure would be worked up to approximately a one-and-a-half-storey building, eleven logs high. This would, in most cases, present a 22-inch-face log from end to end, so that at each end there would be 22 inches, and another log would be put on top. Before chinking could take place the roof and floors would be added. This added a much needed stability to the exterior log walls. The top one or two courses are often joined at the corners by a 45-degree-angle piece

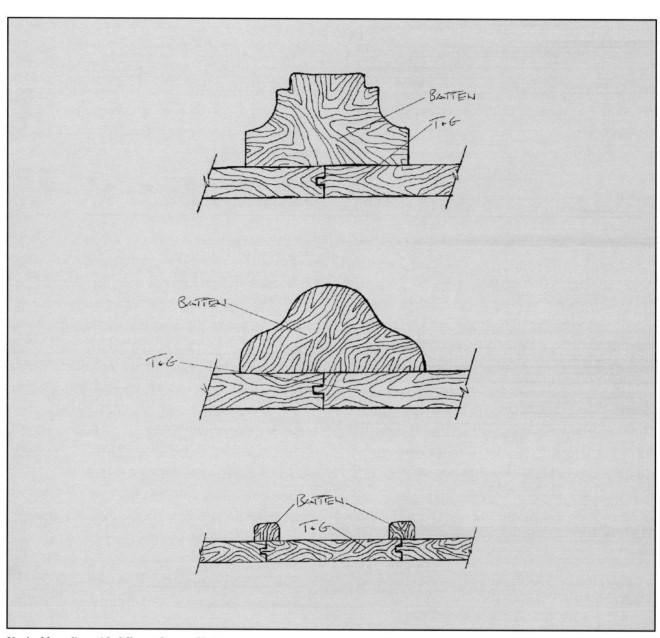

Vertical boarding with different forms of battens.

made of steel or wood, which resembles a pin driven in and down through the log and then across the join. These pins held the top logs together until the rafter system and roof were in place. The entire structure was, at this point, quite unstable and, in fact, as the rafters and roof were going up, these pins or corner 45-degree-angle pieces prevented the entire structure from peeling apart.

The stability in a log house comes from its roof system and the floor joists that are running from side to side. This, in turn, holds the entire system together. Although theoretically not doing any work, the floor and wall systems, if done in a traditional manner (i.e., with plank), help hold the building together. If other floor and wall elements are removed, the sheathing will hold the remaining elements together. Theoretically the sheathing could not hold everything together, but occasionally it does.

Restoring a log house in its original location is a similar process to that of restoring any wooden house. Ensure that the foundation system is secure, that there is no moisture close to the base logs, that there is waterproof shedding on the roof, adequate chinking within the walls to shed water, adequate sash and doorways, flashing in the roof system — in fact, everything that is needed to prevent moisture penetration.

There is an ongoing problem with chinking. In its traditional form it was a soft mortar which crumbled with the continual movement of the log walls. This crumbling would require new chinking approximately every five years. This problem has been rectified, to some degree, by a product called Permaseal, which is commercially available. It is a chinking system that doesn't shrink and has an elasticity about it, which lends itself to the movement of the house.

If one acquires a log house and it must be moved, there are two ways of doing it. The first method is to hire a competent contractor who specializes in log buildings. This will relieve you of all the problems that can occur during the disassembling process. Whoever engages in this operation must be certain to follow the following process. If the log building is already stripped to its logs, it will now need to be tagged, photographed and drawn, so that every element of the building is recorded. All numbering must be sequentially coded to the drawings that are provided at the time. No reconstruction or restoration problem is more severe than not getting the coding right on a log building.

Early in my career a client contacted me; he had been given a log building which was then dumped on his property. A third party had already tried, unsuccessfully, to put it together. The client thought that there was no problem — just a bunch of logs, already cut into shape, that had to be reassembled. After four of our men, fully trained in log construction, spent endless hours sorting and moving, trying to reconstruct with what was there, we had to retire from the project. The client was very frustrated with this problem, and called in another crew who, of course, experienced the same problem. Finally the client agreed to let them cut brand-new dovetails, change the dimensions and literally build a brand-new log building. Clear and thorough documentation is imperative.

While you record and document your log building, a new foundation should be constructed, according to the dimensions that the building dictates, at your new site. The building has now been stripped of all material except for the logs. Metal tags are securely attached to each log, with the correct coding, corresponding to your drawing. These tags are folded over so that in transit they are not scratched, rubbed or knocked off. Do not spray-paint the logs: how would you get the paint off? Use metal tags to document the process.

A crane is then brought in with a flatbed trailer, and one by one, the logs are lifted off and placed on the trailer. When you arrive at your new site, the logs are then systematically removed from the truck and placed in the reverse order from which they were taken. Probably one of the most important things to remember in re-erecting a log building is that it comes apart as a rectangle or square, and it must go back together as a rectangle or square. Not only must all the corners line up, but the diagonals must also line up. The 90-degree angles should be accurate. You can often assemble the logs and everything will fit, and then you will find that you have a serious bow. At that point you may actually have to engage a bulldozer to very gently shift the entire structure over in order to line everything up. If you don't get the walls straight then nothing else will fit. The roof rafters and the floor joists will not go back into place.

It is also important to remember, as you are re-erecting the logs, that the floor beams must be installed. Once the logs are erected and the top logs are pinned together, the roof system can go on. Once again this will be the rafter system. Often it will not be the original system because one may be upgrading the R-value to one of the contemporary standards of today. It will be more cost-effective to use a new roof system than to try and adapt the old one. Once the roof is in place, the floors can be installed. By this point you have floors, exterior walls, roof — all of your major structural components — in place.

Only when you have reached this stage can the chinking take place. Up until this time the structure has been quite unstable, with a large amount of movement taking place. If chinking had occurred before this time, much of it would now be cracking and breaking. Along with the chinking you will install all the weatherproofing for the house: exterior shingles, sash replacement of window, replacement of exterior doors. Gable ends which have been framed during roof construction can now be sheathed and clad, preferably in the original style. Often in Ontario a board-and-batten gable end was employed. The soffit-and-fascia can be finished in a traditional style as per the drawings. Porches, summer kitchens, etc., can now be constructed around the log house. At this point you will also be ready to deal with the interior. It will be like dealing with the interior of any period home.

An excellent example of sill and clapboard restoration in a late 19th-century structure in Key West, Florida.

New board and batten siding, shellaced knots and a finish coat help restore this turn of the century frame house in Key West, Florida.

This well-maintained Queen Anne style house in New Brunswick, is as charming and useful today as it was 100 years ago.

A well-maintained log house. Note log replacement in the #7 log, front facade.

Re-chinking is an ongoing necessity in log houses.

Tight dovetails help ensure structural stability.

CHAPTER FIVE

Interiors

The interior wooden components of a house are as follows: the floors, the walls, the trim, the mantels and the doors.

Like the exterior door, interior doors are subject to a vast array of damaging incidents. Obviously the weather is not one of them. Interior doors are often built in the same manner: that is, as a working device within a framework. If you strip away all of the surrounding walling and flooring, you will find an independent element made up of a framework, a series of moldings and a jamb that the door would be hinged and locked into. If you remove that unit and the sill intact, you will have a complete component making up a free-standing door. Before anything is done, refer back to your photographic documentation of the house, detailing the door, its position, swing, deterioration (if any), paint forms and hardware.

What are the areas of deterioration? Floor settlement may have led a previous owner to remove and trim the door, the hardware may have been changed, there may be general abuse from humans and animals (Fido may have left his ingrained scratch work on the wood). To restore, as with the exterior door, try to keep as much of the original as possible. Once again, use compatible materials

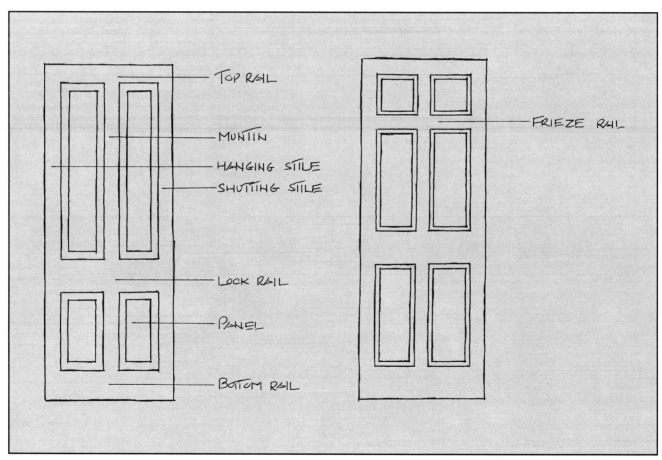

Internal door.

A 19th-century kitchen.

Neo-Classical joinery frames a gracious music room.

and try to do as much as possible in situ, without taking things apart. To be effective you might be wise to consult with a cabinetmaker who can do the work properly.

The first use of wood within the structure is, of course, the floor, whether a rudimentary plank or a fine parquet flooring. Each floor has its own problems in terms of restoration. We will separate them into two categories: the common floor and the fancy floor. The common floor would consist of pine, narrow birch, ash or oak boards. The more ornate or fancy version would consist of parquet or inlay floors.

As with most of the house's features, there is a utilitarian, as well as a decorative, component to the construction. Early floors were often planks that were washed at the end of the day, often with a sand covering. These plank floors were either face-nailed to the floor joists below, or joined face-nailed and held together with a spline or strip of wood that ran through a groove on either side of the flooring plank.

As paints became common in the nineteenth century, floors were painted. This was done for a few reasons: it helped keep the floor clean, it offered a protective layer to reduce wear and it could act as a decorative device. In floors that are made of softwood, you must ask the question: how extreme do you want to be in the refinishing or restoring of this floor? Many pine-plank floors have a fair amount of wear, and harder knots within that flooring project above the actual finish of the floor. For us, the charm of that feature far outweighs the joy of having everything uniform, clean and spanking new. The wear marks are most interesting, they are part of the patina. However, we are not interested in a floor that is worn to such an extent that it becomes problematic in day-to-day usage.

Pine floors that are somewhat thin can often be restored or rejuvenated by screwing plywood on the underside of them. One must make sure, in turn, that the screws do not go through the floor. This step provides a stability to the floor and a rigidity while giving it the flexibility of movement. Be careful not to screw the reinforcing boards too tightly up to the joists. Planks that are extremely worn, or that have been cut or vandalized, can then be removed and randomly restored in keeping with the rest of the flooring pattern. When they are finished they should match rather than stand out from the finished floor.

Hardwood floors have their own set of problems. Like the pine, they were often built on a subfloor. By the mid nineteenth century they were often of tongue-and-groove construction, toenailed to each other as they were placed. Long-lasting if well maintained, they can be as good today as they were a hundred years ago. Worn sections naturally occur in heavy traffic areas, and around doorways. Again, you can remove the offending area and replace it with compatible new wood.

The basic or common floor can usually be repaired by a conscientious tradesperson. Fancy floors, however, require a skilled craftsperson. As with other areas, everything should be documented. Elements should be noted on your plan, photographed and coded.

Before refinishing a floor some questions must be asked. After washing and cleaning the floor you will have to decide how it should be refinished. Will you resand and repaint? Will it be stained and varnished? What will that finish look like? Will this be a period finish, and will fancy painting be applied? The actual process of refinishing will be discussed in Chapter 6.

Interior walls were sometimes made of planks which ran between two strips nailed into place. Variations of this occurred in a form of sheathing in which an actual molding was used to disguise the joint. This was referred to as the cockbead or shadow molding. Evidence of its use can be found into the mid nineteenth century, in rural Ontario.

Paneling itself, although not widely used until the late 1700s in English-speaking North America, had been used by both the Spanish and the French settlements in the 1600s. The Finnish botanist, Peter Kalm, noted while visiting New France in 1749:

The interior partition of boards and occasionally of columbage, created two functional divisions of space in the farmhouse. One for sleeping, and the other for cooking and eating.

As with most things, practicality came before decorative device. The wainscot panel was born to protect from the abrasion of chairs against that part of the wall. Therefore, a wooden panel with a wooden cap on it, or chair rail, was constructed around the room at approximately 36 inches from the floor. When people moved their chairs against it no damage would be done to either the plank wall or to the actual plaster, which was new and somewhat expensive.

The raised panel, or floating panel, is basically a panel cut from one section of wood and applied in a way that allows it to float within a surrounding framework. This is necessary in order that it may weather the movement of the house due to moisture conditions. If it is rigid, and this sometimes happens with painting over the years, the panel movement becomes impeded and the panel will split. It is imperative, therefore, that these panels do not get caked up with paint or nailed into place.

The actual trim, or baseboard, was often applied before the plasterwork. As with any interior woodwork until the mid nineteenth century, baseboards and trim must be restored as per the original. Once again, go back

OPPOSITE AND ABOVE

The machine age was not without aesthetic appeal. This survives from Brockville, Ontario, circa 1880.

either plank or lathing, called ribbon or accordion lath. This accordion lath was a plank split with a froe and hammer, and pulled apart as per an accordion. Although this practice is reputed to have ended in the late 1700s, we can still find it throughout New England and Eastern Canada until the late 1800s. The lath was nailed onto the interior framework, and then the plaster was applied to that after the rest of the interior and molding was set into place. By the mid nineteenth century, standard machine-cut lath was widely used throughout North America in domestic construction.

As you are contemplating the detailing involved in the finishing of your home, it is essential to consider the evolution of the building in terms of hardware and the technology from which it came. Without nails, one could not build a house in the way that we see it in contemporary terms. We must remember that a timber-framed house, for the most part, required no nails. Blacksmiths were the main source of metal materials at that time, and as the century progressed their main occupation would have been providing tools for building and agriculture, until the mechanization of the Industrial Revolution began. By that time, the blacksmith had more time to offer for the tedious process of making handmade nails. In the late 1700s, nails were produced from a rod which blacksmiths acquired from an ironworks. These rods were cut to the length of the nails required and heated and hammered into a tapered strip. The head was then hammered into some type of irregular shape.

In the early nineteenth century, a nail-cutting machine was invented. It was still a hand-done process but now involved a machine with a guillotine knife that alternately, after each cut, produced a tapered piece of metal. The smith then hammered the head to give it the finished look that it required.

to your original recorded information, photographs and plans, and document exactly what trim and baseboard were used. Trim areas and baseboards, wherever possible, should be restored, and offending or broken areas replaced or spliced into place.

Stud walls, in the post and beam tradition, evolved into the frame walls that we know today from the early nineteenth century. These stud walls were covered with

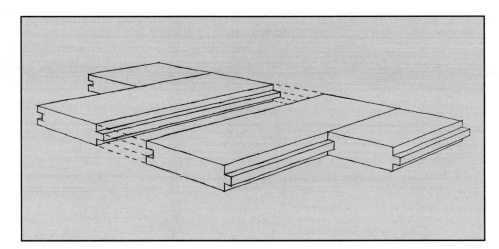

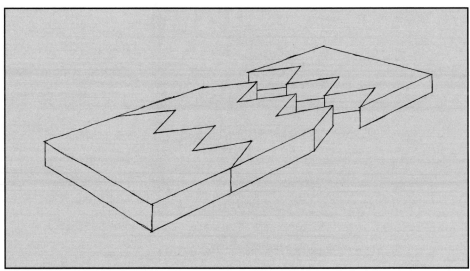

By this time the technology was there to do plaster work. The problem was the lack of availability of nails to install the lath. Only the wealthy could afford to have plaster walls in their subsequently finer homes. The blacksmith was kept busy making assorted handmade hardware for the home. This would include door latches (both Suffolk and Norfolk), hooks and eyes, and any type of hardware that was needed. In many cases, however, during this transitional period, handmade was married to machine-made. For example, a blacksmith-made Norfolk latch might be fitted to a machine-made backing plate. As the technology developed, so did the evolution of the latches and other hardware. By October 15, 1903, in the *Universal Design Book* of the Lawton Co. of Saint John, New Brunswick, we find a great variety of machine-made hardware — nails, sash moldings, etc.

By the early nineteenth century a nail-making machine that also put a head on the nail was introduced. The process evolved with time, and by 1870 wire nails

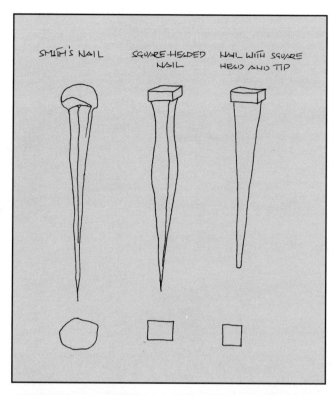

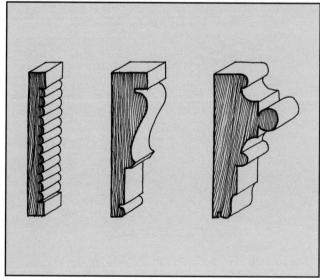

were introduced. These were mass-produced in great numbers. (The earliest wire nails were used around 1830, but they were brought into common use around 1870 in balloon-framed houses.) Mass production would have evolved by 1880, as the Industrial Revolution had finally taken hold. Many of the elements of houses and their components were now machine-made.

When replacing interior moldings, profile gauges should be used. Sometimes one finds that the profile gauge cannot deal with the dimension of the period trim, especially with some baseboards. In that case you will have to make a profile and draw it out as accurately as possible on a piece of cardboard. Then place the cut-out profile against the existing baseboard to check for accuracy.

Very rarely will mills have existing knives in stock to recut period woodwork. In most larger metropolitan areas there will be one mill that specializes in this work, but you will have to pay dearly, because they actually grind the profile to mill the trim required. There is another alternative which can be incredibly time-consuming: you can remake the moldings with a hand plane, if a period plane can be found that matches your need. For you this may be a satisfying and enjoyable experience, knowing that you recreated some of the period trim of your home by hand. Our suggestion, in terms of time and efficiency, is that if you are dealing with a large quantity of moldings to be replaced, then take the time and money and have your local woodworking shop create the knives and run the moldings.

Chimneys in early buildings were often made of mud and wood. For obvious reasons (such as their ready combustibility) we won't dwell on their restoration. Furthering their evolution into a masonry element, the fireplace still held a focus within the house. There was a chimney piece, which was the origin of the fireplace

TOP
Nail styles.

BOTTOM
Molding profiles.

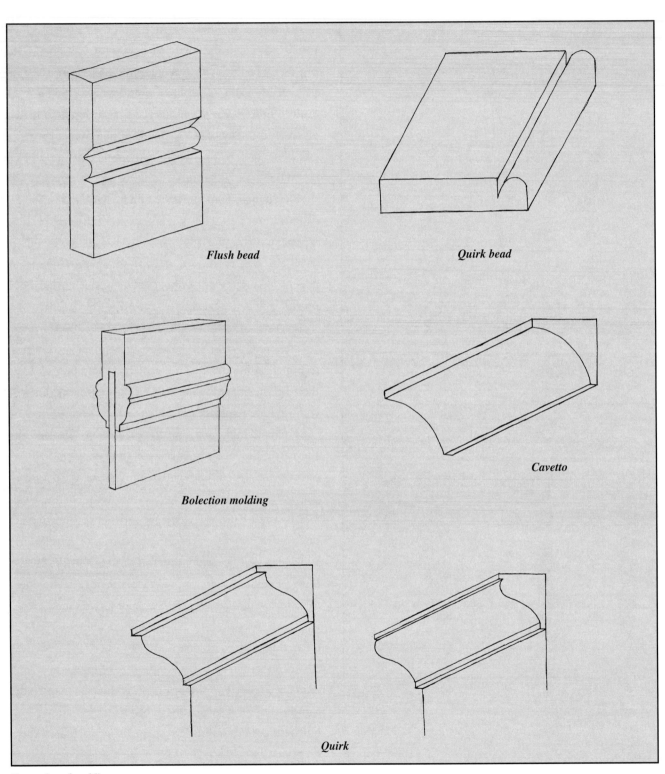

Flush bead

Quirk bead

Bolection molding

Cavetto

Quirk

Examples of molding.

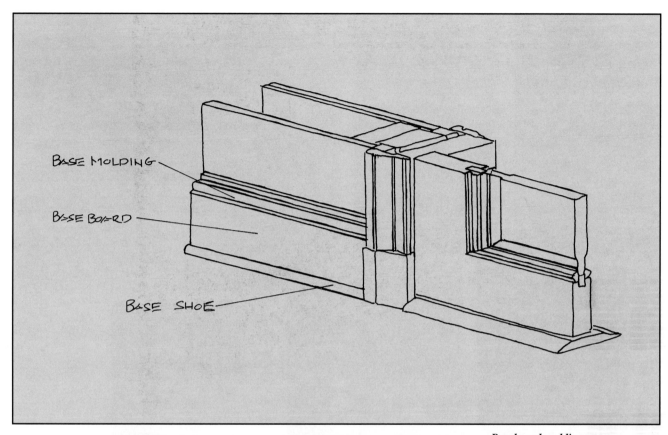

BASE MOLDING

BASE BOARD

BASE SHOE

Baseboard molding.

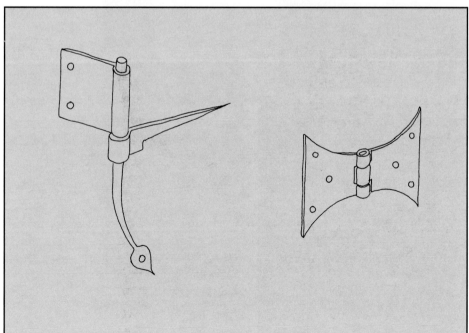

LEFT

A rat tail hinge, early 19th-century Quebec.

RIGHT

Butterfly hinge, early 19th-century New England.

Wherever possible, make use of
existing period hardware.

mantel and which evolved into a panel — becoming, in fact, a paneled wall around the fireplace. The mantelpiece itself was often, and still is, the focal point of the room, and members of the household and their guests could sit enjoying the visual delights as well as the comforts of being close to a warm fire. The fireplace mantel was often one of the prominent ways in which a cabinetmaker could display his art or expertise in wood carving. Samuel MacIntyre of Newburyport, Massachusetts, was probably one of the great builder architects of the eighteenth century, and his mantelpieces are some of the finest that North America has ever seen. A.J. Downing had suggestions as to the decoration of the mantel:

Nothing ... adds to the splendor and gayety of an apartment as mirrors.... The two most ... effective positions for mirrors are as chimney-mantel glasses. A mantel-glass designed to form a whole with the chimney, and reaching nearly to the height of the ceiling, always has a more architectural effect than in any other place.

The mantel does suffer from its own unique problems. Because it is in an area surrounded by warmth, the wood can become charred or damaged, and often detailing is lost by too many layers of paint. The mantelpiece, when possible, should be removed from its area, stripped of paint build-up and the woodwork restored.

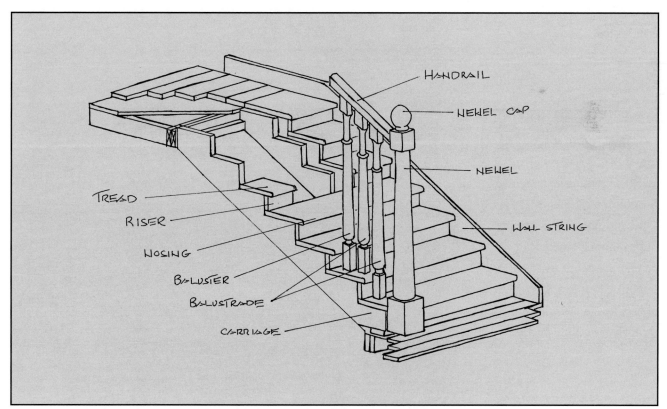

Staircase details.

If you live in a northerly climate you will probably want to make your home somewhat energy-efficient. The addition of insulation to period buildings in the mid twentieth century, although pleasurable in immediate creature comforts and energy-saving costs, often causes major problems to the period building. Inadequate vapor barriers, or no vapor barriers whatsoever, are part of this problem. The insulation is often blown in, which means that the amount of heat escaping through the walls is uncontrollable. Where the heat hits the cold wall on the exterior, moisture is created. This in turn will cause rot within the framework of the wall.

If a house is in extremely good condition — that is, if walls, paneling and insulation cannot be adequately installed within the framework without causing a major disturbance to period features and details, then our suggestion is to insulate the attic and crawlspace or basement only. When installing insulation into the attic, lay down a vapor barrier and then put the insulation bats or loose fill on top of that. Make sure that adequate venting goes through the dormer, gable ends and the soffit-and-fascia. This will not only minimize any type of deterioration, but will also minimize heat loss. Fifty percent of heat loss in a house goes out through the ceiling or roof.

A newly constructed Ontario mantel in the 1830s tradition.

Heating and Insulation

Early buildings often maximized natural sources of sunlight and landscape in order to cater to the creature comforts of living in them. Houses were often situated in a place where natural vegetation or a hill or valley helped insulate or cool the house. A good example of this is a timber frame house that we once occupied. It was built in a valley and surrounded by small trees. In the middle of winter when the temperature outside was 30 degrees below zero, the sunlight that streamed in, combined with the shelter of trees and its situation in the bed of the valley, made the house much warmer than the temperature on top of the hill. There was sometimes a twenty degree difference. Period houses often had twenty percent less

glass to wall ratio in their makeup. Large amounts of surface glass were not there to cause problems. Blinds and shutters and heavy curtains were often used to protect the inhabitants from the blustery effects of cold winds. The window coverings not only kept the cold of winter out, but also the hot sunlight of summer. The windows also served as a practical device for allowing cool breezes in, to aid in the proper functioning of fireplaces and woodstoves, as well as offering welcome relief from a humid summer. Builders of the period house took into consideration the situation of the house in terms of its function. Today we often erect houses wherever it suits us and impose standard mechanical solutions. People in past generations actually employed the landscape to enhance the heating and cooling of their homes. Dark paint would often be applied on the exterior of the house to draw in heat from the sun in winter. The planting of trees was not just done for decorative effect, but to deflect winter winds and summer sun.

One of the major concerns of living in an older structure is the mechanical systems in terms of plumbing, heating and cooling. Wherever possible existing systems may be used, e.g., forced air or hot water heat (radiators). Both are effective. Often when retrofitting these systems you'll find the actual mechanical unit requires updating. New systems employing oil or natural gas are not only efficient and practical but in terms of physical space they take up far less room than the original. Radiators should be bled and the system cleaned out. With forced air heating the ducts should be cleaned out and new vents put in them. Forced air systems have the benefit of moving air around. We have often found that the small fans within a structure used to move air around are very beneficial in the overall heating of a period house, especially those with high ceilings.

It is obvious that mechanical systems will be upgraded, such as for air filtration. Retrofitting the structure is less obvious. Although you're attempting to get rid of cold

Existing exterior cladding and sheathing has been removed to insulate this mid-19th-century braced frame house.

drafts you don't want to seal the house entirely. Not only is this bad for your health, but it's bad for your mechanical systems and fireplaces, which need air to function. When you're caulking and retrofitting windows and doors as mentioned, make sure that there is some play in the system so that air can come in. Whenever possible we try to use the original windows because there is always a little play in them. We don't want them to be perfectly tight.

The easiest areas to insulate are the attic space and the basement or crawl space. The attic space should be insulated by first installing a vapor barrier face down so that if you were in an upstairs room looking up you would have the ceiling of the room, then the lath to which the plaster was attached and then above that you'd have the ceiling framing and then the attic space. The vapor barrier would go on top of that initial framing. You'd then put a bat insulation or cellulose fiber on top of that. This would give you your vapor barrier and insulation. The most important thing to remember in this process is to ensure adequate venting in the attic, which can go out either through the eaves or the gable ends of the building, making sure that the architectural decorative features of the vents are in keeping with the period structure. You can also vent directly through the roof. It is imperative that the air passing through the soffit and fascia and attic space is the same temperature as the outside air. If you do this you will not have a problem. The roof system, the cladding and actual structural system itself will not break down. You'll have a functioning insulated roof system.

When insulating basements or crawlspaces, the process is similar. Either use rigid insulation or frame it in such a way so that your bats can be attached to the framework hanging down from the basement joists. We often take it down and leave it just above the floor system

so that if there is ever a flood or moisture problem in the basement the bats specifically do not become waterlogged and useless. You then employ your vapor barrier on top of that system, which should ensure a warm and cozy basement. Make sure that your ducts and pipes are well insulated. If you are considering insulating the actual walls in a wooden house there are two methods that you can employ. One is the exterior method. This employs the removal of the exterior cladding and in some cases the sheathing, so what is left will be a series of voids. The actual framework, when you're looking at the exterior of the house, will consist of uprights with the lath and plaster coming through. What you will then do is employ a vapor barrier and either foam or bat in your insulation and then reclad the exterior elements. Another method of doing this is to remove only the clapboard and to install a vapor barrier and then attach rigid insulation over the vapor barrier and over the sheathing before reattaching the clapboard. The only problem with both of these methods is that you are not dealing with absolutes. There is always a major chance of rips and tears within the vapor barrier, which will in turn lead to condensation occurring within the wall at different areas, subsequently leading to rotting. The other problem, particularly within the latter system, is that it throws the proportion of the exterior house off because you've added approximately four inches of insulation on top of the existing building, which means that your roof system and all your doors and windows have to be built out. In fact you are changing the entire proportion of the house. It's one of those things to consider. The long term payback of this process is quite expensive. We would recommend that a professional should be involved and serious questions asked if you are going ahead with this process.

Insulating the interior of the house we are loathe to recommend unless it has no rewarding architectural

if the existing one is not adequately installed, painting two good coats of an alkyd paint or an aluminum primer on the ceiling will serve the same purpose as a vapor barrier. This ensures that there is a barrier formed by this paint doing the same thing as a vapor barrier. Obviously it will not be as effective because where the walls go up into the attic there will be an air space and a potential for condensation.

If one intends to use the attic space as a working room, insulation of the floor of the attic is not the recommended way to go. The insulation should be attached to the rafter system, the sloping portion of the roof and held in place either with chicken wire or some type of strapping and the vapor barrier applied to the inside section of the roof system. Before that is done though channels should be built so that air can move from the soffit and fascia system up through the roof area so that we get an air flow within that space. This renders the actual room of the attic a warm insulated room, the roof system insulated and the venting going through a small space between the insulation and the roof sheathing. This venting should be employed coming out through the soffit and fascia system.

As mentioned earlier, one of the most delightful ways to aid in the insulation and cooling of your house is through landscaping. The positioning of trees, porches, overhangs and awnings can have a major impact on

features to speak of. Basically, you have to gut the house. You are removing the plaster and lath, interior moldings, and taking the house back to its shell so that all that is remaining is the framework. Everything within it has been removed. You will then install your bats being aware that you may have to reframe in some cases to accept contemporary bat sizes. Install your vapor barrier and then redo the plaster or drywall. The former is obviously recommended. There is once again the problem that you will alter the proportions of the rooms and for the most part not get much advantage from the actual process. For the cost vis à vis the look we would highly recommend that you do not entertain this process. In insulating a period house, the biggest problem is condensation. Condensation occurs when warm air hits cold air and moisture develops on the first hard surface nearby. Vapor barriers must be placed on the warm side of the insulation, the side facing the heat source. If a period house has been purchased and insulation has already been blown in or bats installed into the attic space and you're not sure if a vapor barrier has been installed or it looks as temperature. It is not so much the coldness of air, but wind penetration, that seems to be a problem with heating period houses. Wherever deflection of wind can occur the problem decreases. Masonry houses (brick and stone) suffer less in this regard than wooden houses, because there are fewer joints, and so fewer areas for the wind to penetrate. Strategic plantings around the house, particularly of the coniferous families, can reduce heat loss by sometimes 20 percent around the period structure.

Kitchens and Bathrooms

Contemporary bathrooms and kitchens pose a different set of problems in a period structure. Venting should be employed in these two areas wherever possible. Because we use bathrooms, showers, and laundry rooms daily, there is a great deal of moisture build-up that never occurred in a period structure, and it is imperative that these rooms be adequately vented.

Contemporary kitchens add their own problems in redesigning or restoring the period house. Often plumbing systems are inadequate for today's lifestyle. When redesigning a kitchen to make it functional for you and your family, once again consider the past. How was the kitchen used? Was there a pantry? Was a table used rather than a counter as a work surface? The placement of a contemporary stove, fridge, sink and work area can often be based on parallels in historical tradition. The overabundance of windows and doors in late 19th century houses means that interesting design concepts can be introduced within that space.

Often one will decide to adapt another room rather than employing the existing kitchens or bathrooms. Often period houses didn't have interior bathrooms, so you should carefully consider where your bathroom should be situated. How easily can the plumbing runs be worked into the present system? Wherever possible the kitchen and bathroom should be worked out in unison so that plumbing runs can be centered and brought down in one area. These can then be built into an existing wall or some type of cupboard or bulkhead created that would be visually in keeping with the rest of the room. Period detailing such as wainscotting can be employed in counters and islands, carrying the period theme through so as not to have jarring changes in the interior design. Period reproduction hardware can often be employed in these areas. Often a summer kitchen would not have an adequate foundation but only a crawlspace. If plumbing runs are to be installed throughout the crawlspace it is imperative to insulate either the exterior perimeter or the interior of the crawlspace, making sure of course that there is adequate stability within the existing foundation for the work that one is about to employ. Sometimes in less harsh climactic conditions, for example, below the Mason Dixon line, it is possible to insulate the pipes rather than the perimeter of the house. It is important to look at joist systems and framing to ensure that any new stove and fridge combinations can be supported in the area that you wish to put them.

When looking at bathrooms and their layout consider the fact that a bathtub full of water plus a person can sometimes weigh 800 to 1200 pounds. Consider the stress of this load on the building system.

Cabinets and work surfaces can often employ period features. We often are inspired by cupboard door designs from the existing doors within the original building or from a structure close in period to that. Counter-tops can employ period details such as marble or compatible alternatives such as granite. Laminated maple counter tops add to the contemporary look of a room.

Often period elements can be used as decorative features.

Period newel post and railing, circa 1840.

ABOVE

Inset window well panels, circa 1860.

RIGHT

An Adamesque detail.

A series of photos showing how wainscot can be reproduced.

CHAPTER SIX

Finishes

Wood is an ideal building material, but its longevity depends on care and protection. This can be provided by substances such as paint, sealer or stain. These not only protect the surface from the ravages of time and weather, but they also enhance the appearance of the surface, becoming the so-called icing on the cake.

Up until 1800 most buildings were painted white, or they were whitewashed. This was usually a mixture of linseed oil and lime, used more as a protective coating than anything else, although obviously the decorative element did come into it. By the early 1800s a small palette of paint, or colors, was being used throughout North America. The color codes on page 142 will serve as a guide for these early color schemes. By the late nineteenth century a broad palette was offered.

Exterior coatings were lead-based. In the process of restoration an oil based, or as we now call it an alkyd-based, paint is our best recommendation. A good quality alkyd paint will deteriorate slowly and shed moisture. When repainting a stark wooden structure, it is important to analyze what color would have been used at any given time. Take scrapings from different elements in the building and then compare them with historic charts of the period. In that way you can create a comparable color scheme. When doing this it is important to photographically record where you took the samples in the house plan. For example, if you photograph the elevations of the house, take your results, combine with scrapings from your samples and then code the photos to your front elevation.

The actual procedure involved in repainting requires a number of steps. First, scrape the remaining or loose paints that have deteriorated from the existing surface. It is very important to clean out or remove paint from architectural details. Over a period of one or two

An ongoing maintenance program is imperative.

Stripping the original finish sometimes reveals a less than pleasant image.

hundred years a great amount of paint will have built up, masking the period detailing. The tools to use are either mechanical, such as scrapers or sandpaper, or chemical (as in chemical stripping). Mechanical tools should probably be your first choice and, if you can proceed without causing damage, a heat gun may be employed. This is a tool that actually blisters the paint off, causing it to flake right down to the surface. Where the paint isn't built up and covering over architectural details, all one needs to do is roughen up the surface so that the new paint will adhere to the old paint.

Before repainting all exterior woodwork should be completely cleaned and primed so that the surface is ready for a new application of paint. Where mildew, molds or fungus are present, it is important to wash the surface thoroughly with a mild fungicide before sanding and repainting. Use a commercial fungicide or a mixture of water, detergent and a small amount of bleach. The

surface should be wetted down before scrubbing the mixture into it. When you are finished, generously hose the area down with a light pressure wash of 100 psi.

Interior painting can be approached in the same manner. It is important to document all rooms, moldings, and wall and floor surfaces. In doing this you will have your floor plans, wall elevations and photographic documentation. These can be married to the color system that you will be using. Here the use of the color window, described below, will be invaluable.

To find out what colors were used where, you can use a simple but effective method called the color window. Place some commercial color remover in a saucepan or dish. Take zero–zero steel wool, dip it into the remover and apply to the surface in a circular motion. (Make sure that you are wearing rubber gloves to avoid burning your hand.) The remover permeates the paint layers. As it goes through the layers to the wood, apply the steel wool in a circular motion. This will cut through the different layers, feathering out the number of paints that were on the actual section of wood. Further dating may be possible by comparing these layers with the other details of the house's history. Oil-based paints do darken with time, and the real shade that you pull out of this color window will often be lighter than those discovered.

In paint work inside the house, the main areas of deterioration are the same as they are for the house in general. The ultraviolet rays from sunlight break down the paint over time (although ultraviolet destroys latex slower than oil or alkyd). The presence of moisture from high humidity or condensation will cause everything from dry rot and wet rot to warpage. General dirt, surface grime and the usual abrasions that occur from day-to-day living will cause the paint to break down.

Technology has altered the chemical make-up of finishes, although visually they have changed very little. Whitewash was an inexpensive material used during the seventeenth and right up until the twentieth century. It was made from water and slaked lime. Sometimes salt and glue were added as binders. The negative aspect of whitewash is that it eventually flaked off and it was coarse in texture — not a particularly elegant look for the formal interior.

Distemper and calcimine paint were also used from the mid eighteenth century until the 1930s. Opaque watercolor paints — made from calcium carbonate, tinting pigments, water and glue — were cheaper than oil and easier to work with. This finish was often used as a sealer for oil paint on fresh plaster. Oil-based paints were made of oil, linseed oil, white or red lead, and color pigments. Milk-based paints were introduced in the early nineteenth century. They were made from a mixture of slaked lime, skim milk, linseed or nut oil, and pigment.

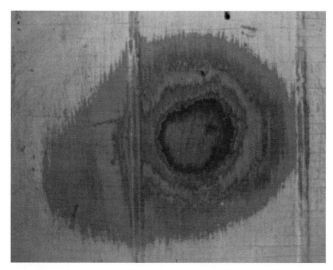

ABOVE & OPPOSITE
Items used to prepare a color window.

There are three methods of removing paint from interior woodwork.

1. The abrasive method, which means using sandpaper or a power sander.
2. Heat devices — heat guns, blow torches, heat lights.
3. Chemical stripping.

Sanding with a palm or orbital sander is about the extent that one would want to get into mechanical sanding within a house. Hand-sanding with sandpaper would be the best way to prevent damage to existing woodwork. Heat guns used within a house are extremely dangerous. Paint itself is flammable under heated conditions, and this method is not advisable. However, if you find it necessary to use this approach, exercise extreme caution. It is imperative to have a fire extinguisher or bucket of water handy. Make sure that nothing is left burning or plugged in after you have finished, for obvious reasons. Chemical stripping can be broken into two categories:

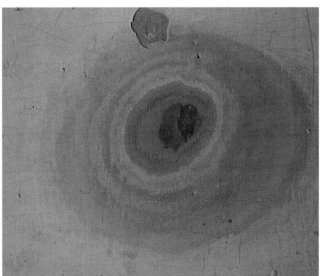

Employ a heat gun to remove paint from a fluted column.

1. Caustic removers, which are lye-based. They are commonly used for commercial purposes, such as stripping tanks.
2. Organic solvent strippers, which are methylene chloride-based. These are usually used in interior work.

The importance of safety in all of these methods should be quite obvious. Each method presents health hazards. When a chemical stripper is used, the area to be stripped is coated and left for approximately five minutes. This should be done in a temperature between 65 and 85 degrees Fahrenheit. As the chemical softens the paint, scrapers, knives or other devices are used to remove the paint until you get to layer number one,

closest to the wood. Then coarse steel wool is used to remove the remaining layer.

Let us describe the process of refinishing a floor, since this is usually the largest area of wood found in a house, and it is often one area that most concerns the owner of the house. When done properly it is a sight to behold; when done carelessly it might inspire one to call in the carpet installers. Strip off the wax and any other material and then lay on your new finish as you would any woodwork. To sand an existing plank floor, an edger or orbital sander (such as a small hand sander) and a rotary disc drum sander must all be employed. Warning: this can be an extreme health hazard because early paints were often lead-based. When sanding them, paint dust fills the air, creating a toxic situation. Wear a mask and

Lay out the color materials in order to work out your color scheme.

An 1840 Recipe for Whitewash

Put lumps of quick-lime into a bucket of cold water and stir it about till it is all dissolved and mixed. It should be about as thick as cream. A pint of common varvish (which can be procured at a cabinetmaker's for a trifle) — will make it stick like paint. Instead of water to mix the lime with, skim milk (which must be perfectly sweet) will make the whitewash very white and smooth, and prevent it rubbing off easily — put on with a very long-handled brush made for the purpose — when it is quite dry, it must be gone over with a second coat, and if the wall is very dirty or has been colored with yellow ocher, a third coat — may be necessary.

vent the area totally. All windows and doors should be left open and fans employed to blow the dust out. You should also check legislation in your area regarding the use of paint strippers and lead paints.

Step 1: Take the edger and sand the edges of the room, going around all areas adjacent to the baseboards.

Step 2: Employ the drum sander, going up and down in line with the planking runs of the existing floors. Wherever you find dips you may need to go into these with the edger or hand sander, feathering it in. This will be done by trial and error and is not usually a pleasant task.

Step 3: The finished floor should be drummed again. Go sequentially from coarse to medium and then to fine.

When the floor is totally stripped and everything vacuumed and wiped clean, you can begin the fun of rolling on your finishes. Remember to use an alkyd-based paint on your floor, and a minimum of five coats so that it can endure the wear of the household.

The decision to repaint a period house is often the first temptation. Unfortunately, it often becomes the last temptation, as your enthusiasm for the project wanes. Repainting is really the total icing on the cake, and great care and attention should be paid to the process, because that is what you will finally live with. It will be rewarding and will show all the finery and hard work that has taken place up to that time. As discussed before, wherever possible original color schemes should be used, whether plain or fancy.

Using the described methods, we will have created a plan for the color scheme.

Whether using an alkyd, oil-based or latex finish, the application is more than important. Work through wall by wall, one at a time. Don't stop painting in the middle of a wall, do it one wall at a time. Start with cutting the edges and then roll or, if you are fanatical about the look of the actual surface, brush on the entire finish. Obviously you are using the brush to give the same type of finish that was originally applied.

Adequate venting should be employed throughout the house when repainting. As to the number of coats: as previously discussed, there will usually be a residue of a number of coats there. If you are starting afresh, it is worth priming it with shellac (cut with 50 percent methyl hydrate), a primer coat, then two finish coats. If there are fancy coats involved in this process, you will need more coats on top of that.

The chart on page 136 describes various finishing techniques and products ranging from stains, oil finishes, waxes, lacquers and varnishes, and alkyds and latex paints.

The newly finished floor is saturated, due to overly zealous use of preservative.

HOMEMADE DISTEMPER

- whiting (one 3 kg bag for small room)
- decorators glue size (containing alum to check mold)
- make glue size up (follow directions)
- Leave it to cool, until it has hard jelly-like consistency.
- Heat it by placing its container in a larger container of water over heat. When it is warm and runny it's ready.
- Next stage: bucket, cold water, powder color for tinting, spoon and larger bucket of hot water.
- Fill small bucket half full with cold water and add whiting to peak 4 inches above water. Leave for $1^1/_2$ –2 hours, stir.
- Dissolve color powder in small amount cold water and slowly add to whiting mix until desired color.
- Stir until color is even, then add glue (warm) and mix thoroughly. It should be like thick paint.
- If it begins to stiffen, place container in larger bucket of hot water. It will not keep for more than a day or two.

Alternatives to distemper:

- use glaze of very thinned oil based paint
- undercoat over eggshell base (mid sheen oil-base)
- or use wash of latex thinned with water applied on a clean flat base.
- 3rd method: use wash of color and water, add a bit of latex paint for body. More than one coat can be used; make sure that each dries before applying the next. Apply each coat quickly, or preceding coat will be dislodged.

Problems with Paint and Wood

Paint		
Problem	**Cause**	**Solution**
Inappropriate quality or color of finish	Later applications of incorrect finish or stain	Remove existing finish and apply new, historically appropriate finish
Wood character and detail obscured	Buildup of finish layers	Remove existing finish and apply new, historically appropriate finish
Blotchy and inconsistent finish	Age, wear, light	Remove existing finish and apply new, historically appropriate finish
Wood		
Cracked or split wood	Dryness, moisture	Insert wood or epoxy patches, or fill with wood putty or filler sticks. Longterm: determine causes of damage and install humidifier or dehumidifier as appropriate.
Buckled or warped wood	Dryness, moisture	Straighten wood with wet towels and weights. Longterm: install humidifier or dehumidifier as appropriate.
Dry or wet rot	Condensation	Remove rotted area and fill with wood filler or wood or epoxy patch. Longterm: install dehumidifier or air conditioning, cover dirt cellar or crawl space with plastic tarps.
Insect infestation	Deterioration of protective finish, condensation	Remove rotted area and fill with wood filler or wood or epoxy patch; renew or reapply protective finish. Longterm: determine cause and source of infestation.
Panel shrinkage	Dryness	Glue panel in place. Longterm: install humidifiers.
Peeling veneer	Moisture, heat, dryness	Glue damaged sections. Longterm: install dehumidifier, air conditioning, shades, awnings.
Lifted or blistered veneer	Moisture, heat, dryness	Slit and insert glue. Longterm: install dehumidifier, air conditioning, shades, awnings.

PAINT DEFECTS	PROBLEM	REMEDIAL
Chalking	Surface paint powders from external exposure or poor vehicle in paint	• scrub down • seal • reapply paint
Blistering	Moisture or resin pockets trapped, causing blisters	• scrape • seal • reapply
Blooming	A surface mist of milkiness caused by too much moisture or cold temperature during application	• wipe down • reapply gloss finish
Bleeding	Previous materials in the surface appearing through new paint coat	• scrape • seal with shellac or aluminum prime paint • repaint
Flaking	Peeling or lifting of paint from lack of adhesion due to paint application to dirty surface	• strip • clean dirty surface • reapply
Sagging or Curtaining	Paint unevenly applied, causing a slump-like look to wall	• sand vigorously • reapply paint
Grinning	Inadequate coating due to poor paint quality, bad application or incorrect thinning	• reapply new coatings
Cissing	Paint retreating from some areas due to a foreign substance on the work surface	• strip to wood • reapply paint as to surrounding surfaces
Surface Cracking Grazing	Finish coat being applied over a previous coat which was not fully dry, or over a soft undercoating	• strip • totally recoat

TOXIC WOODS

This list includes woods that are known to cause allergic, toxic, infectious or respiratory reactions. Although researchers point out that not everyone is sensitive to these woods, they warn that woodworkers should be particularly cautious when sanding or milling them. The category "respiratory ailments" includes bronchial disorders, asthma, rhinitis and mucosal irritations; "skin and eye allergies" includes contact dermatities, conjunctivities, itching and rashes.

Respiratory ailments	Skin and eye allergies		Respiratory ailments	Skin and eye allergies	
X		Arbor vitae (*Thuja standishii*)	X	X	Makore (*Tieghemella heckelii*)
	X	Ayan (*Distemonanthus benthamianus*)	X	X	Mansonia (*Mansonia altissima*)
	X	Blackwood, African (*Dalbergia melanoxylon*)	X	X	Obeche (*Triplochiton scleroxylon*)
X	X	Boxwood, Knysna (*Gonioma kamassi*)	X	X	Opepe (*Nauclea trillesii*)
	X	Cashew (*Anacardium occidentale*)	X	X	Peroba rosa (*Aspidosperma peroba*)
X	X	Cedar, Western red (*Thuja plicata*)	X	X	Peroba, white (*Paratecoma peroba*)
	X	Cocobolo (*Dalbergia retusa*)		X	Ramin (*Gonystylus bancanus*)
	X	Cocus (*Brya ebenus*)		X	Rosewood, Brazilian (*Dalbergia nigra*)
X		Dahoma (*Piptadeniastrum africanum*)		X	Rosewood, East Indian (*Dalbergia latifolia*)
X	X	Ebony (*Diospyros*)		X	Satinwood, Ceylon (*Chloroxylon swietenia*)
X	X	Greenheart (*Ocotea rodiaei*)	X		Sequoia Redwood (*Sequoia sempervirens*)
X		Guarea (*Guarea thompsonii*)	X		Sneezewood (*Ptaeroxylon obliquum*)
X	X	Ipe [lapacho] (*Tabebuia ipe*)	X		Stavewood (*Dysoxylum muelleri*)
X	X	Iroko (*Chlorophora excelsa*)		X	Sucupira (*Bowdichia nitida*)
X		Katon (*Sandoricum indicum*)		X	Teak (*Tectona grandis*)
X	X	Mahogany, African (*Khaya ivorensis*)	X	X	Wenge (*Millettia laurentii*)
	X	Mahogany, American (*Swietenia macrophylla*)			

DOCUMENTATION
EXAMINATION — CLEAN — REPAIR — PRIME — RESURFACE

Finish	Makeup/Uses	Negative	Positive
Shellac	• Sealer/finish • Made from resin from Asiatic LAC beetle • White and orange	• Will watermark • Will darken with age	• Excellent product • Can pump up existing color finishes • Easily cut with methyl hydrate • Can be removed easily with no lasting damage
Varnish Type A	• Traditional varnish (resin-derived)	• Will darken with age	• Cut with turpentine • Durable, repairable
Varnish Type B	• Plastic varnish	• Do not use	• Do not use
Varnish Type C	• Water-based varnish	• Raises wood grain • Need more coats to achieve same thing	• Non-polluting • Water-soluble
Lacquer	• Synthetic finish (nitro-cellulose base)	• Brittle • Will not stand in areas of constant abrasion (doors, etc.) • Often hard to remove	• Much like shellac, but harder
Dry oil stains	• Linseed oil	• Will darken with age • Soaks into wood; cannot remove • Sticky in humid areas	• Cheap • Natural
	• Tung oil		• Reasonable degree of moisture and abrasion resistance
Wax	• Beeswax • Carnauba • Mix with mineral spirits for workability	• Not moisture- or heat-resistant	• Ideal final coating over shellac or other paint finishes

Finish	Makeup/Uses	Negative	Positive
Alkyd paint	• Oil-based, cut with mineral spirits • Eggshell, gloss, semi-gloss or flat		• Will probably match existing paint types in project • Removable • Adaptable • Good wearability
Latex	• Water-based paint • Eggshell, gloss, semi-gloss or flat	• Hard to remove • Medium-wearing • Often incompatible with existing finishes	

WOOD FINISHING CHARACTERISTICS

Name	Relative Hardness	Grain	Finish	Name	Relative Hardness	Grain	Finish
Ash	Hard	Open	Requires filler	Hemlock	Soft	Close	Paints fairly well
Alder	Soft	Close	Stains readily	Hickory	Hard	Open	Requires filler
Aspen	Soft	Close	Paint	Mahogany	Hard	Open	Requires filler
Basswood	Soft	Close	Paints well	Maple	Hard	Close	Takes any type of finish
Beech	Hard	Close	Poor for paint, takes varnish well	Oak	Hard	Open	Requires filler
Birch	Hard	Close	Stains and varnishes well	Pine	Soft	Close	Takes any type of finish
Cedar	Soft	Close	Paints well, finishes well with varnish	Spruce	Soft	Close	Can be painted, stained or finished natural
Cherry	Hard	Close	Requires filler	Teak	Hard	Open	Requires filler
Chestnut	Hard	Open	Must be filled, not suitable for paint finish	Walnut	Hard	Open	Requires filler, takes all finishes well
Cottonwood	Soft	Close	Good for paint finish				
Cypress	Hard	Close	Takes paint or varnish, finishes well				
Elm	Hard	Open	Not suitable for paint, requires filler				
Fir	Soft	Close	Can be painted, stained or finished natural				
Gum	Soft	Close	Can be finished with a variety of finishes				

Notes:
1. "Open grain" is associated with varying pore sizes between springwood and summerwood.
2. "Close grain" is associated with woods having overall uniform pore sizes.
3. "Hard" and "soft" refer to relative hardness of wood, and have no relation to hardwood or softwood.

EXTERIOR FINISHES FOR WOOD PRODUCTS

General Use: Lumber, Siding and Panel Products				
Type of Finish	**Preparation of Surface**	**Sealers and Primers**	**Application of Finish**	**Characteristics**
PENETRATING FINISHES				
Preservatives			Brush one coat of water-repellent preservative onto surface.	Imparts mildew and decay resistance; some protection from ultraviolet light destruction, depending on pigment content; easy to maintain.
			Brush a solution of fungicide onto surface; best method is to add fungicide to finish.	May tend to leach out with rain.
			Pentachlorophenol (five percent to ten percent solution) may be added to stain; alternatively, wood may be pressure-treated with preservatives.	Preservatives desired but not absolutely necessary for eastern white or western red cedar.

Type of Finish	Preparation of Surface	Sealers and Primers	Application of Finish	Characteristics
Pigmented Stains	Sand or scrape wood to flat, clean surface; if new wood, no preparation required.	None required.	Brush latex or oil-based stain onto surface; working area should be small enough to maintain a wet edge; one or two coats applied according to manufacturer's recommendations.	Easy to apply; attractive finish for even rough surfaces; easy to maintain; choice of semi-transparent or oblique finish.
SURFACE FINISHES (RARELY USED)				
Alkyd paints	None required.	None required.	Two coats of specially formulated shingle and shake alkyd paint, supplied by brush.	Flat finish; covers all but extreme surface irregularities.
Latex paints		Specially formulated sealer required; factory-primed shingles and shakes are available.	Two coats of latex paint applied by brush.	Covers all but extreme surface irregularities.
Weathering and bleaching agents		None required.	Follow manufacturer's directions.	
Synthetic varnishes		None required.	Same as for general use.	Not recommended; see "General Use."

Type of Finish	Preparation of Surface	Sealers and Primers	Application of Finish	Characteristics
Madison Formula			Brush one coat of Madison Formula onto new wood.	Semi-transparent oil-based stain intended for western red cedar; imparts water repellency and mildew and decay resistance; contains wax, which leads to refinish problems.
Oil			One coat of oil, applied by brush.	Not recommended.
SURFACE FINISHES				
Solvent-based paints (including alkyds)	Sand or scrape off badly deteriorated finish; if new wood, no preparation is required.	Apply knot sealer or shellac to knots and pitch streaks; apply oil-based primer to new wood.	Painting should be done in dry weather with temperatures above 7 degrees Celsius; paint following the sun around the house, staying one side behind the sun; apply one or two coats (depending on color) by brush.	Alkyd paints overcome blistering and excessive chalking associated with traditional oil-based paint; recommended if color is required; alkyd trim paints should be used above masonry; solvent-based paints with other synthetic resins are available.

Type of Finish	Preparation of Surface	Sealers and Primers	Application of Finish	Characteristics
Latex paints		Apply knot sealer or shellac to knots and pitch streaks; apply oil-based primer as undercoat or special latex primer over previous coats of oil-based paints.	Follow application instructions above for solvent-based paints; apply two coats of latex paint by brush over primer.	Easy to apply; adhere well to damp surface; dry rapidly; easy equipment cleanup; chalk-resistant; slower to erode than oil-based paints; thinner surface film, and therefore less levelling off of surface irregularities.
Synthetic varnishes	For refinishing, scrape off loose flaking materials, sand area, wash wood surface and stain bleached areas to match the rest of the wood; if new wood, no preparation required.	None required.	Three coats of synthetic varnish are applied by brush to new wood; fewer coats required for refinishing.	Refinishing required about every two years; finish allows penetration of ultraviolet, which degrades film and wood surface; results in darkening of wood color.

SHINGLES AND SHAKES (WESTERN RED OR EASTERN WHITE CEDAR)				
Type of Finish	Preparation of Surface	Sealers and Primers	Application of Finish	Characteristics
PENETRATING FINISHES				
Pigmented stains			Immersing shingles or shakes in stain (semi-transparent or opaque) is best technique; refinishing done with a brush.	See section on "General Use"; rough surface of shingles and shakes readily absorbs stain.
Madison Formula	Same as for "General Use."	None required.	Apply as for other pigmented stains.	Madison Formula specifically formulated for eastern white or western red cedar.

SAND PAINT

As cut stone was thought to be more elegant than wood as cladding, wood was often cut to simulate ashlar. The use of sand paints as a coating further accentuated and heightened this illusion. A contemporary comparative method is described below:

- Use a compressor-operated glitter gun and a blend of garnet sands.
- Use white lead and linseed oil paint as a base tinted with Burnt Umber, Burnt Sienna and synthetic Yellow Ocher, all ground in linseed oil.
- Spray sand into wet paint.

A historic method is described as follows:

"All the wood work outside is to be painted 3 good coats with the first quality pure white lead and linseed oil paint & sanded twice at the time [of] putting on the two last coats and made to imitate Portland stone."

Directions for Mixing and Painting the Following Colors for Outside Work

WHITE

For the first coat, use two thirds Spanish White and one third white lead; grind and mix in the kettle as before directed. When this is thoroughly dry for the second coat use equal quantities of Spanish White and white lead; for the last coat, use white lead only.

CREAM COLOR

Add to white as above directed, in the proportion of one pound to three pounds.

DIRECTIONS

To prepare oils for outside work

Use only brass or copper vessels — place red lead in the proportion of one pound to four gallons of oil, at the bottom of the vessel. Add the oil; then let them simmer or boil very gently over a slow fire, until clarified. When the red froth ceases to rise on the top, the oil is clarified and fit for use.

To prepare paints for outside work

Take a smooth iron kettle of middling size, and an iron ball weighing from 12 to 24 pounds. Suspend them in some convenient place by a rope or chain. Put into the kettle four to six pounds of Spruce Yellow or English Ocher, well ground. The yellow tinge may be varied at pleasure by increasing or diminishing the proportion of the Spruce Yellow or English Ocher.

STRAW COLOR

Lay on the first two coats white, or slightly tinged with yellow. For the last coat, to every ten pounds of white lead, add one pound of Spruce Yellow or English Ocher, well ground and mixed.

ORANGE COLOR

Add to straw color one pound of red lead for every ten pounds of the above mixture.

PEA-GREEN

For the first coat, use white tinged with Lampblack. For the last two coats, add Verdigris in the proportion of one pound to every ten pounds of white lead.

PARROT GREEN

Prime with white tinged with lampblack as above directed. For the last two coats, use five pounds of white lead, one pound of Verdigris and four ounces Spruce Yellow.

GRASS GREEN

Prime as above. For the last two coats, use equal quantities of Verdigris and white lead. Add to the three last mentioned colors Spirits of Turpentine in the proportion of half a pint to each gallon of paint.

RED

For the first and second coats, use two pounds of red lead and ten pounds of Spanish Brown, well ground and mixed. For the last coat use four pounds of red lead, eight pounds of lead, and eight pounds of Spanish Brown. For a richer and more durable color, finish with Venetian Red only.

SLATE

To equal quantities of white lead and Spanish White, add Lampblack in the proportion of one common sized paper to each twenty pounds of the above mixture. The shade may be varied at the discretion of the painter.

BLACK

To every ten pounds of Spanish White, add ten papers of Lampblack. For beauty and duration, use Lampblack only well mixed with oil.

For painting sashes, only oil and white lead should be used.

Doors may be painted according to the foregoing directions. Should other colors be prepared, the directions for inside work may be followed.

DIRECTIONS FOR PAINTING INSIDE WORK

Preparation of Oil

Use a brass or copper kettle. Cover the bottom of the vessel with red lead, laid smooth and even. In the proportion of half a pound to each gallon of oil, boil the same over a slow fire, until the oil will singe a feather: then let it cool, and add one gill of Copal Varnish or Spirits of Turpentine to each gallon of oil.

Paints must be ground dry, and perfectly pulverized. For small quantities, use a marble and muller.

When thoroughly pulverized, mix the white lead with oil and grind it separately from the coloring ingredients.

In like manner mix the articles which you propose to use for making the color as Prussian Blue, Stone Yellow, Venetian Red, etc. after pulverized, with your boiled or clarified oil. Grind them in oil separately from the white lead. After the materials are thus thoroughly ground in oil, separately, mix them together according to the following directions. Grind them together giving them a consistency to work free as before directed and they are then fit for use.

The quantities hereinafter stated are to be understood, after the several paints have been mixed with and ground in oil.

Prepare the room for painting by filling the cracks and nail holes and covering the nail heads with putty, that the surface may be smooth and even.

For sizing, dissolve one pound of glue in one gallon of boiling water. Add two pounds of Spanish White. When cold, and well mixed, lay it on carefully and even with the grain of the wood, with a clean brush.

DIRECTIONS FOR MIXING AND PAINTING THE FOLLOWING COLORS FOR INSIDE WORK

PEARL COLOR

To one pint of white lead add one teaspoonful of Prussian Blue and one teaspoonful of Spruce Yellow.

ICE COLOR

To one pint of white lead, add one teaspoonful Rosin, one teaspoonful Verdigris and half a teaspoonful of Lampblack.

LIGHT STONE COLOR

To one pint of white lead, add two teaspoonfuls of Prussian Blue, four do. of Spruce Yellow and one do. of Umber.

SEA GREEN

To one pint of white lead, add one tablespoonful of Verdigris and one do. of Spruce Yellow. Mix and grind them well together. If upon experiment it should be too light, add of the coloring ingredients at discretion.

PRUSSIAN BLUE COLOR

To five pounds of white lead, add one ounce of Prussian Blue of the "best quality." If the quality be inferior, the quantity must be increased. In laying this paint, use a half-worn brush and press the brush harder than in laying other colors.

A Navy Blue may be made by adding 2 oz. of Prussian Blue, and a Sky Blue by adding half an ounce of Prussian Blue to give pounds of white lead.

DARK STONE COLOR

To six pounds of white lead, add eight ounces Yellow Ocher; and half a gill of Lampblack.

RED COLOR

May be made with either Vermillion, red lead, Rose Pink or Dutch Pink, ground in oil. Venetian Red, Spanish Brown and Red Ocher are coarser paints.

PURPLE COLOR

Is made with Rose Pink and Prussian Blue in equal quantities.

CLARET COLOR

Is made with white lead, 3 parts, and Spanish Brown, 1 part, well mixed and tinged with a small quantity of Lampblack.

CHOCOLATE COLOR

Is made with Spanish Brown and Lampblack and may be varied at discretion.

MAHOGANY COLOR

Prime with Spruce Yellow. When thoroughly dry, add to the yellow a small quantity of white lead, say four ounces lead to one pound yellow, and lay the second coat. For the third coat take a sufficient quantity of Stone Yellow pulverized; heat it on coals in iron taking care to stir it constantly until it changes to a red color, then let it cool. Mix and grind it with clarified or boiled oil, and it will be fit for use. Then for shading the work, take Umber pulverized and prepare it by heating as before until it changes to a darker color. Then mix and grind it in oil. When both are prepared lay the third coat and immediately shade it with the Umber, that the colors may more easily blend together.

For shading use a graining or flat brush, and lay the paint in imitation of Mahogany wood, of which have a sample handsomely polished before you. When thoroughly dry, finish with a coat of Copal Varnish neatly laid with a clean brush.

RED CEDAR COLOR

Prime with red lead and white lead in equal quantities. For the second coat use the same. For the third coat, to four pounds white lead add two ounces Vermillion well ground and mixed. Immediately, while the third coat is green, shade with India Red in imitation of the grains and knots of cedar. For shading, the India Red should be well ground and mixed, and placed on a pallet or pane of glass, that it may take easily with the brush.

MARBLE COLOR

First and second coats may be laid with white lead and Spanish white in equal quantities; for the third coat use white lead only. Shade with Prussian blue, ground and mixed with oil, and laid on with a graining brush while the third coat is green; in imitation of clouded marble, finish with Copal Varnish.

CHERRYTREE WOOD

For the three first coats, use white lead and yellow Ocher in equal quantities. While the third coat is green, shade with umber prepared as before directed, and finish with Varnish. Any other imitations of clouded or shaded work may be done in a similar manner by varying the foregoing directions according to the judgment and taste of the painter.

DIRECTIONS FOR MAKING FLOOR CARPETS OR OILED CLOTH

Canvas or common tow cloth is sewed with a flat seam, of the dimensions required, and nailed firm upon a floor. Then it is wet with water evenly and thoroughly. Before dry, it is primed with any common color. When this coat is dry, a second coat is laid with the same. The third coat is painted with a stone color, and when dry, the carpet is turned and painted with any convenient color on the other side. When dry, the carpet is turned back, any flaws or cracks which appear are filled with putty, and the surface is made smooth and even.

With a chalk line a margin six or eight inches wide is struck. The remaining part is divided into squares or diamonds of which one-half, taking them as placed in a diagonal line succeeding each other, are painted white, and the other half black. The squares may be clouded at pleasure. The margin may be ornamented as clouded, with little labor by using paper patterns.

CLOCKWISE FROM ABOVE

Color sampled blocks being prepared.

Stripped, primed, two coats: painting the period door.

Original stenciling in the VanSycle house in Jerseyville, Ontario, circa 1830.

Late 19th-century stencil.

LEFT

Details make the project complete.
Late 19th century.

BELOW

Crotch grain mahogany finish.

Original stenciling, Scotch Line, Lanark County,
Ontario.

Paint removal with a heat gun.

CHAPTER SEVEN

Additions and Landscaping

Additions

Period domestic houses often do not fill all the spatial needs that one requires in a contemporary household. Therefore, a quandary exists: do you move to a bigger house or put on an addition? If an addition is selected, what type of addition? As previously mentioned, the preservation of the historic house is ideally in keeping with its past use and architectural style. What do we do when it comes to adding something new today? There are two schools of thought on this subject: the first suggests that we acknowledge the fact that it is the late twentieth century and therefore design something in keeping with architectural trends and standards of today. The other choice is to recreate something that would be suited to the period that the house is being restored to; for example, if it was a one-and-a-half-storey cape house, then an ell off the rear of the building, or a one-and-a-half-storey wing off the building, would be in keeping with the original. One might also adopt a compatible element — clad with clapboard, 12-over-12 windows or a roof with wooden shingles. If, on the other hand, one chooses an alternate, then it is possible to use similar building materials in the scale and proportion of the original, to marry in an extremely attractive and harmonious addition. The key word here is "proportion." Wherever possible, the addition should be unobtrusive and suit the original structure as much as possible. In no way should any addition or new structure impose on the original.

Additions should be built of like materials: if a building is clad in clapboard, then it would be appropriate to use a clapboard cladding on the addition. The same applies to windows. You may decide not to use 12-over-12 windows, but merely to create spaces that occupy the same proportional element that the original windows did. If you do tend toward the preservation method or toward the reconstruction of a period-type addition, then I think it is only responsible to make note that this is, in fact, an addition. Do not try to conceal this truth, but instead allow yourself, or your designer, to make a creative statement that affirms the reality.

Coupled with this philosophy is the practice of using recycled wooden elements. This practice was common in the eighteenth century and it should be today. Ronald F. Frazier notes in the magazine *Antiques* that

> [a]bout the time the lean-to was added, twelve-over-twelve windows were hung in the front of the house, replacing the original leaded casements, and the thrifty Yankees hung the old casements in the lean-to at the back.

You may incorporate items of a technical nature, or visually appealing architectural components that were saved from the wrecker's ball when another period building was being dismantled. There are treasures to be discovered in the wrecker's yard. Salvage yards, demolition sites and companies that specialize in the recycling of period wooden elements are now relatively common throughout North America. These elements may include wooden floors, hand-hewn beams, windows, doors, etc. Often these components can be installed into your home in a way that may not be historically correct, but can be visually appealing. For example, a hand-carved door may be hung on the wall as a piece of sculpture. There have been many exciting examples of this kind of creativity in North America in the past five years.

OPPOSITE
This fence complements the outstanding Victorian frame house.

Architectural landscape elements must also be maintained if we wish to avoid deterioration.

Landscaping

The established wooden house is, of course, situated on a landscape, and the attention to this area is as important as the attention you give to the house itself. The location, the outbuildings, the vegetation, the fencing and the surrounding walkways all play as vital a role in the final look as does the hardware used in the dining room.

North American landscape design is divided into four major periods:

1. The colonial (ancient style), which started around 1620 and ended approximately 1775. During this time, North America evolved from being the storehouse for European appetites into an entity in its own right.
2. The gardens of the new nation — 1776 to approximately 1860.
3. The Victorian period — 1860 to 1900.
4. The early twentieth century — 1900 to 1930.

The earliest gardens, set in what is called the "ancient style," were made up of well-cultivated blocks of garden separated by paths running between them. This style can be noted throughout history — from the Dark Ages to mid medieval times and right up to the seventeenth century. These rectangular spaces were bordered by planks or logs and the gardens, vegetable and floral, put within them. The raising of beds above the actual grade was thought to have been better for drainage and aeration. There is some truth to this idea, except when there are dry spells and then, of course, the garden dries up faster without watering.

All gardens in this time were surrounded with fences, which fell into three categories:

A mid nineteenth-century board-and-batten fence.

1. Variations on the stockade style or the pole fence. This created a walling effect by driving poles into the ground, pointed end down. They were then bound together with a cross member or binding.
2. The picket fence — a fence using poles and smaller pieces called pickets — evolved from the pole fence. The pickets were kept close together so that farm animals could not wander into the garden or away from the farm.
3. A variation on this same theme is the horizontal rail or board fence. These were easier to erect and more economical because they required less material.

Walkways or sidewalks were either gravel, wood mulch, sawdust or planks set in either a tort, horizontal or vertical fashion. These planks would lay on sleepers set in the ground.

The period from 1776 to 1840 saw the birth and widespread popular influence of actual designers and landscape gardeners. Two of the most renowned designers of this time were J.C. Louden and Andrew Jackson Downing. The expertise of Downing, a designer of houses, ranged in scope from the general landscape and ornamentation of the house into the actual art of landscaping around the home. He transformed wooden

elements in the landscape from utilitarian objects into aesthetic statements.

Fencing, trelliswork and greenhouses all evolved during this period. This use of the garden and landscape as an addition to the house continued through to the Victorian period. Great excesses, such as ornamental fences, summer houses and greenhouses, not only employed wood in their construction, but also iron,

which was introduced during the mid nineteenth century.

Landscape design in the early twentieth century gained as much from the past as from the contemporary. Bernard McCann, whose seed house had begun in the late 1700s, and whose influence extended to J.C. Louden and Andrew Jackson Downing, still had a major influence throughout the early twentieth century. In

A well-maintained and restored gatepost and gate.

great houses a sense of eclecticism was born, coupled with the traditions of the previously mentioned personalities. Extensive travel had opened North American eyes to gardens throughout the rest of the world. The influence of European gardens and landscapes became widespread and combined with the growing movement toward individualism; the house and surrounding gardens became an eclectic personal statement of one's creativity and taste. The upper classes went so far as having statuaries, ponds and major avenues throughout their estates. These took on a very architectural quality and were somewhat formal, harkening back to the colonial period but bringing with them various aspects of the European and Oriental traditions. The estates were ringed with walls of stone, iron or wood, and often had large gates or gateposts.

The average person's house simply had a front yard with foundation plantings and borders surrounding the house with a variety of flowers. These flower borders also surrounded the rear and front yards. There would be a driveway and a rear drying yard where the domestic chores of the house were carried out. There was a service yard, which was probably in a smaller house or adjacent to part of the drying yard, in which the trash was put out, firewood or coal was delivered or stored, and the vegetable garden or fruit trees were established.

Upon commencing a restoration, the same plans should be made for the landscape as for the house itself. A file of research and documentation should be created. A photographic record should be kept of all plantings, beds, wood extrusions, trees — anything around the house, including fencing and walkways. Any type of historical documentation — catalogs, early photographs that might be found in the home or with neighbors, or town documents — should be researched and considered in the preservation process. The movement of the sun across the property should be noted. Diaries or scrapbooks, along with paintings and the local archives, will all help document the type of foliage and landscape elements that were used in that area and perhaps even on your specific property.

One house that we purchased still had the remains of an amazing garden that the original owners had created. We were delighted to see the house mentioned in a yellowed newspaper clipping, written by one Gladys Blair, found in one of the cupboards:

> *Many of her [Mrs. Harold Kidd's] paintings adorn the walls and reveal a talent of exceptional dexterity.*
>
> *The garden at the rear is built in terraces, with a grape arbor and former croquet lawn included. It too was one of Mrs. Kidd's hobbies, and there are still traces of lily pools, fountains, and masses of flowers.*

Stories from the locals told us of a time when our garden had been the setting for many a wedding or other special occasion. It had been the garden that people came for miles to see. Some were able to tell us exactly what had been planted where. Eventually we were able to restore areas of the garden by getting clippings of perennials from neighbors. What was so amazing for everyone involved in this process was that the clippings, in some cases, came from fully mature plants grown from clippings that had originated in our garden. Now that is truly the spirit of recycling!

Period documentation aids restoration. Note fences and work areas.

The ultimate back garden experience.

The porch can be as much a part of the landscape as the garden.

Period picket fence, circa 1840.

Afterword

The increasing popularity of recycling existing sources is a positive, if somewhat basic, principle for our present society. Reusing and adapting existing architectural structures should be part of this process. Up until the mid twentieth century, most structures were built within a tradition of longevity. Skills and materials were considered important factors, even without intense and rigid legislation. As the "throwaway" attitude of the twentieth century evolved, so did diminished standards in trade, excellence and quality of materials used. This has occurred despite the sometimes rigid rules imposed by building codes and commissions. Today vast tracts of suburban houses are granted 25-year mortgages, a duration partly based on the life expectancy of the structure. The often inferior materials and craftsmanship in the average domestic structure render it unrestorable in the future. The assumption is that it will be knocked down and another will be built in its place.

The person who purchases an older home has been granted an opportunity to not only preserve part of our cultural heritage, but to also preserve resources that are rapidly being depleted.

Architectural preservation should not be a separate or distinctive part of the domestic building industry. It should be the model from which we establish contemporary standards. This will only happen when financial institutions, and the bodies that establish construction guidelines, educate themselves and develop awareness of the concrete value of our architectural history.

Glossary

ARCADE: A range of arches supported on piers or columns. Hence *Arcade posts* if made of timber.

ARCADE-PLATE: Longitudinal horizontal beams carried on the arcade posts of an aisled hall to support the rafters of nave and aisle. Square-set, then developed into a *purlin*.

ARCH-BRACE: A curved timber across the angle between principals, etc., and tie-or collar-beam, two forming an arch below the latter.

ARCHITRAVE: Lowest component of the three primary divisions of the entablature in a classical order: also, molding around window and door openings.

ASHLAR-PIECE: A short timber rising vertically from the inner end of the sole-piece to the underside of the common rafter.

ASTRAGAL: Also known as a bead; a convex, semicircular molding: one of eight classical molding shapes.

AUMBRY: Cupboard.

BACK HOUSE: Any building in the connected farm complex located between the kitchen and the barn. Also called the ell or shed. *Back house* may also refer to a privy or outhouse located in these buildings.

BALLOON FRAMING: A method of wood-frame construction in which the studs extend in one piece from the foundation sill to the top plate supporting the roof.

BALUSTER: A small column supporting a hand-rail.

BALUSTRADE: A row of balusters topped by a rail, forming a railing or fence.

BASEBOARD: A molded board placed against the wall around a room next to the floor, to conceal the joint between the floor and wall finish.

BATTEN: A narrow strip of wood used to cover joints between boards or panels, or to hold boards together.

BATTER BOARD: Boards set a right angles to each other at each corner of an excavation, used to indicate the level and alignment of the foundation wall.

BAY: The space between major structural posts, as found in barns. The most common New England barn is three bays wide and three bays deep.

BAY WINDOW: Projecting window, usually at ground level.

BEAD: A small round molding.

BEAM: A horizontal structural member — usually wood, steel or concrete — used to support shapes.

BEAM POCKET: A notch formed at the top of a foundation wall to receive and support the end of a beam.

BENT: The transverse framing section in a New England barn, usually having four posts and erected as a single structural unit.

BEVEL: The sloping surface formed when two surfaces meet at an angle which is not a right angle.

BIG HOUSE: The first or front building in the connected building complex containing the parlor and bedrooms.

BLIND NAILING: Nailing in such a way that the nailheads are not finally visible on the face of the work.

BOARD AND BATTEN: Type of wood paneling or exterior wood cladding consisting of flat boards joined with battens, usually in a vertical position.

BORNING ROOM: A popular name for the small bedroom adjacent to the kitchen in a typical Cape Cod house. While births occurred there, the term does not appear to have widely used before 1920.

BOTTOM PLATE: The lower horizontal member of a wood-frame wall, nailed to the bottom of the wall studs and to the floor-framing structural members.

BRACE: Subsidiary timber of a roof, inserted to strengthen the framing and prevent racking and bending.

BUILT-UP ROOF: A roof covering composed of three or more layers of roofing felt or fiberglass saturated with coal, tar or asphalt. The top is finished with crushed stone, gravel or a cap sheet. Generally used on flat or low-pitched roofs.

BUTT JOINT: Any joint made by fastening two components together without overlapping.

CALCIMINE PAINT: Also spelled "kalsomine" in the nineteenth century; a distemper paint made of tempera colors, water and sizing.

CASING: Finish woodwork enclosing the opening of a door or window, usually molded or cut in a particular architectural style.

CAULKING: Caulking is used to seal gaps which inevitably exist between building elements, particularly between the window frame and wall. Since these gaps change in size with seasonal temperature changes or movement in the building, the caulking must be elastic.

It must also adhere well to the surfaces on which it is being applied (some caulks adhere better to wood than to metal), and resist the effects of the sun's rays (ultraviolet radiation) and the effects of changes in temperature.

If the gaps is large, the opening is first filled with a substance which serves as a bed on which the caulking is applied.

Traditionally, oakum (tarred hemp) was used although today it has been replaced with fibreglass or polystyrene foam.

When the caulking is going to be painted, it is important to choose a caulk and paint which are compatible.

CHAIR RAIL: Horizontal molding at the height of chair backs to protect walls from being scraped; used alone or applied to the tops of dadoes or wainscots.

CHAMBER: A room located on the second floor, usually a bedroom.

CHAMFERED MOLDING: Molding with a beveled edge.

CLAPBOARDING: A series of boards set up on a sill, each tongued on one edge, grooved on the other, to fit into its neighbor.

CLOSE-STUDDING: Walling of timber posts set little more than their own width apart, with plastered panels between.

COB: A wall made of unburnt clay mixed with straw.

COLLAR BRACE: A horizontal beam tying together a pair of truss blades, or rafters, usually at or about half way up their length. There may be one to three collars to each pair.

COLLAR PURLIN: A horizontal beam with supporting collar.

COLUMN (Latin *columna* = post): A vertical support to an arch, consisting of a base, circular or octagonal shaft, and capital.

COMMON RAFTERS: One of a series of rafters extending from the top of an exterior wall to the ridge of a roof.

CORNER BEAD: A metal strip placed on external corners before plastering, to protect, align and reinforce them, in gypsum board finish, a strip of metal or wood fixed to external corners, to protect them from damage.

CORNICE: In common usage, a projecting molding below the edge of a roof.

COVE: Concave under-surface.

CROWN-MOLDING: Molding serving as the corona or crowning member of a structure; most often used at the junction of wall and ceiling.

CRUCKS: Primitive truss formed by two main timbers, usually curved and set up as an arch or inverted V. Each cruck is called a blade, and a pair may be cut from the same tree.

CUPOLA: A small ornamental structure placed at the crest of a house roof. A less ornate structure paced on a barn for ventilation was called a ventilator.

DADO: Decorative or protective treatment of the lower part of a wall to a height of three or four feet.

DADO-RAIL: Molding on top of the dado.

DAMP-PROOF COURSE: A damp-proof material placed just above the ground level in a brick or stone wall, to prevent ground moisture from seeping up through the structure.

DISTEMPER PAINT: Opaque water-based paint made with tempera colors, whiting and sizing; also called calcimine paint.

DOORYARD: The outside area adjacent to the kitchen and the major barn door and used for farm work activities.

DORMER WINDOW: A vertical window with its own gable and individual roof, in the slope of a roof; usually lighting a sleeping apartment, hence the name.

DOUBLE GLAZING: Two panes of glass in a door or window, with an air space between the panes. They may be sealed hermetically as a single unit, or each pane may be installed separately in the door or window sash.

DOVETAIL: Tenon shaped like a dove's spread tail or reversed wedge, fitting into corresponding mortice and forming a joint.

DRESSING: Term used in joinery applied to any molding or finishing.

EAVES: The overhanging edge of a roof.

EDGE-GRAIN: Lumber that is sawn along the radius of the annual rings or at an angle less than 45 degrees to the radius is edge-grained; this term is synonymous with the quarter-sawn.

ELL: Any building extending outward from the main or big house, usually an L-shaped arrangement. On a connected farmstead, the ell includes all the buildings linking the big house and the barn.

END GRAIN: The face of a piece of lumber which is exposed when the fibers are cut transversely.

EQUILATERAL: A pointed arch formed on an equilateral triangle, i.e. the radii equal to the span.

FACE NAILING: Fastening a component by driving nails through it at right angles to its exposed surface.

FASCIA: A plain, flat, horizontal band often used on architraves.

FASCIA BOARD: A finish member around the face of eaves and roof projections.

FEATHER-EDGED: A tapered edge; an element triangular in section.

FENESTRATION: A window arrangement.

FIELD: The upper portion of a wall, between the dado and cornice.

FIELDED PANEL: A raised panel.

FILLER: Also known as a listel or annulet; a plain, narrow face used to separate other moldings.

FINISHER: A carpenter or housewright employed for finish work on architectural details such as windows, doors, staircases, and paneling

FIREPLACE SURROUND: Wooden molding encasing a fireplace opening.

FLASHING: Sheet metal or other material used in roof and wall construction to shed water.

FLOORING: Material used in the construction of floors. The surface material is known as finish flooring while the base material is called sub-flooring.

FLUTING: Vertical channels of rounded sections cut in shafts of columns or pilasters.

FOOTING: The widened section, usually concrete, at the base or bottom of a foundation wall, pier, or column.

FOUNDATION: The lower portion, usually concrete or masonry and including the footings, which transfers the weight of and loads on a building to the ground.

FRAMER: A carpenter responsible for structural framing and rough carpentry work.

FRET: Also known as a Greek key; incised, painted or applied ornament of thin lines arranged continuously in interlocking rectangular forms.

FURRING CHANNEL, FURRING STRIP: Wood or metal spacers attached to the structure of a building to provide a level surface for finishes.

GABLE: The upper triangular-shaped portion of the end wall of a house

GABLED HIP: Hipped roof with small gable above.

GAMBREL: A roof with a double slope, the lower one steeper than the upper.

GIRT: Any major horizontal structural component supporting ceilings and floors.

GOTHIC: The architectural style of medieval Europe. In America, *gothic* is associated with the revival of this style between 1830 and 1890.

GRADE (lumber): To separate lumber into different established classification, depending upon its suitability for different uses. A classification of lumber.

GRADE: The surface slope; the level of the ground surface around the foundation wall. To modify the ground surface by cut and fill.

GRAINING: Also known as "faux bois"; a simulated wood finish, generally used for inferior woods to create the impression of finer wods.

GUNSTOCK POST: A major vertical member wider at the top to accept horizontal members. Also called a flared post.

HALF-LAPPED: Refers to the joint at the intersection of two wood components where half of the thickness of each of the two pieces is removed, so that they form a flush surface when overlapped.

HAMMER POST: A short vertical post rising from the inner end of a hammer beam to the principal rafter.

HEADER (framing): A wood component at right angles to a series of joists or rafters. When used at openings in the floor or roof system, the header supports the joist or rafters and acts as a beam.

HIP: The sloping ridge of a roof formed by two intersecting roof slopes.

HIP-RAFTER: The rafter which forms the hip of a roof.

INDIAN SHUTTERS: Sliding paneled window covers concealed within the walls of many colonial houses. Often assumed to be for protection against Indian attack, they were actually built for insulation and environmental control.

INSULATION: Material used to resist heat transmission through walls, floors and roofs.

JACK RAFTER: A short rafter that spans from the wallplate to a hip rafter, or from a valley rafter to the roof ridge.

JAMB: The side post or lining of a doorway, window, or other opening.

JOINER: A carpenter or cabinetmaker responsible for interior finish work and paneling.

JOINERY: The name given to all trim and finishes in architectural woodwork that are framed or fitted together, especially on the interior; distinguished from carpentry, which includes rough framing and timber work. Joinery usually includes stairs, doors, windows and dressings; also wood coverings (e.g., paneling) for rough timber.

JOIST: One of a series of horizontal wood components, usually of two inch thickness, used to support a floor, ceiling or roof.

KING POST: A vertical post extending from a tie-beam to the apex of the roof.

LANCET: A point arch formed on an acute-angled triangle, the radii greater than the span.

LAP: A timber of diminished thickness which overlaps another.

LATH: A building element made of wood, metal, gypsum, or fiberboard, fastened to the frame of a building to serve as a plaster base.

LATHING: Thin, narrow strips of wood nailed to structural walls and ceilings to provide a bonding surface for plaster finish.

LINENFOLD PANELING (Latin *Lignum undulatum* = wavy woodwork): Decoration with appearance of a fold of linen, derived from a molded rib multiplied and stopped.

LINTEL: A horizontal beam or stone over a doorway, window or fireplace.

LONGHOUSE: A building of long rectangular plan with living-room(s) and byre under one roof, with a common entrance.

MARBLEIZING: Also known as "faux marble"; a painted imitation of the color, sheen, and veining of marble.

MITER JOINT: A joint formed by cutting and butting two pieces of board on a line bisecting the angle of their junction.

MITER: Junction of two timbers at an angle of 45 degrees.

MOLDING: Element of construction or decoration used to create varieties of contours and of light and shadow and to indicate and hide joints in masonry, wood and plaster. Molding was generally used to mark the boundary between different features, such as the architrave and frieze, or between different components of the same feature, such as the shaft of a column and capital.

MORTICE: A cavity cut in the end of a timber to receive the tenon.

MORTISE-AND-TENON: Wood jointed where one piece of wood has a rectangular recess called a mortise to receive a rectangular tenon projecting from the end of another piece of wood.

MULLION: A vertical bar dividing the lights of a window.

MUNTINS: Short, vertical intermediate framing components between rails, such as in doors and paneling.

NEWEL: Central pillar round which wind the steps of a circular (newel or turnpike) staircase or vice, made up of the rounded projection of each step; also the principal post at the angles of a dog-legged or wall staircase, into which the handrail is framed.

NOTCH: A V-shaped indentation in an edge or across a surface.

OGEE: A pointed arch of double curved sides, the upper arcs convex, the lower concave.

PAINT: A composition of four elements: 1. solid pigment particles which give us colour; 2. the Vehicle or liquid portion, which includes 3. a binder which makes it stick, and 4. a solvent which spreads it.

PANEL: A large, thick board or sheet of lumber, plywood, or other material. A thick board with all its edges inserted in a groove of a surrounding frame of thick material. A portion of a flat surface recessed or sunk below the surrounding area, distinctly set off by molding or some other decorative device. Also, a section of floor, wall, ceiling, or roof, usually prefabricated and of large size, handled as single unit in the operations of assembly and erection.

PEDIMENT: A triangular low-pitched gable over a classical portico, or over doorways, windows, etc

PEDESTAL: A molded block set beneath a column or pilaster divided into three main parts; the base, the dado or die and the surbase, cornice or cap.

PIAZZA: A porch or veranda inspired by Italian examples

PLASTER: A structural post resembling a column (with a square section), engaged or attached to a wall.

PLATE: A major horizontal framing component located at the junction of the vertical posts of the wall and the sloped rafters of the roof.

POINTED, TWO-CENTERED, OR DROP: An arch struck from centers on the springing line

POST: A major upright structural component.

PRINCIPAL RAFTERS: The pair of inclined timbers that also serve as enlarged common rafters.

PRINCIPALS: The main inclined timbers of a roof truss on which rest the purlins which support the common rafters.

PURLIN: A major roof-framing horizontal beam running parallel to the ridge, and supporting smaller common rafters or vertical sheathing.

PUTTY: Putty is an adhesive compound. Traditionally it has been made with white lead or powdered chalk mixed with a binding agent, generally double-boiled linseed oil. Putty hardens as the oil oxidizes, a process which can be accelerated by the presence of white lead or organic substances such as egg white.

There are now other synthetic compounds available for use as putty. Aluminum and steel windows generally require the use of special putties although traditional formulas are still generally used for cast iron or sheet metal sashes and frames.

QUEEN POST: A pair of vertical posts standing on the tie-beam and supporting the side-purlins.

QUIRK: A sharp V-shaped incision in molding.

QUIRK (OR QUIRKED) BEAD: A bead with a quirk on one side, as on the edge of a board, so that it appears to be separate from the surface on which it is planed.

RABBET: A groove cut in the surface along the edge of a board, plank, or other timber. The recess in a brick jamb which receives a window frame. Also the recess in a door frame to receive the door.

RAFTER: One of the components of a roof, usually of two-inch thickness, designed to support roof loads, but not ceiling finish.

RELIEVING: An arch, often rough, placed in the wall over an opening, to relieve it of super-incumbent weight.

RIDGE: The peak of a roof, or a structural component at the peak.

RIDGE BEAM: A horizontal structural component usually two inches thick, supporting the upper ends of rafters.

RIDGE BOARD: A horizontal component, usually

inches thick at the upper end of the rafters, to which these rafters are nailed.

SADDLE BOARDS: A fascia board at the junction of the roof and the gable wall. Also called a rake board.

SALTBOX: A colonial house form with two stories in front, one storey behind and a gable roof, with the rear slope longer than the front slope.

SCARFED JOINT: A joint in which two pieces of timber are bevelled or notched, so that they overlap without an increase in thickness, and then pegged.

SCREW JACK: A rotating screw-operating device for lifting heavy loads such as houses.

SEALER: A liquid applied directly over uncoated wood for the purpose of sealing the surface.

SEGMENTAL: A single arc struck from a center below the springing line.

SEMICIRCULAR: A single arc forming half of a circle from the springing line.

SHAKE: A shingle split or sawn from a block of wood and used for roofing and siding.

SHEATHING: Covering boards encasing the framing members of a building. On houses, these boards are covered by clapboards or finish siding, while on barns the sheathing might be left exposed.

SHED ROOF: A sloping roof with is surface in one plane.

SHINGLE: A wooden roofing tile made of cleft oak.

SHOE MOLD: For interior finish, a molding strip placed against the baseboard at the floor; also called base shoe, or carpet strip.

SHOULDERED: Lintel on corbels which are concave on the underside.

SIDING: In wood-frame construction, the material other than masonry or stucco used as an exterior wall covering.

SIDELIGHT: Narrow vertical windows place on both sides of an exterior door.

SILL: The horizontal component forming the bottom of an opening such as a door or window,

SILL PLATE: A structural component anchored to the top of a foundation wall, upon which the floor joists rest.

SMOKE PIPE: A pipe conveying products of combustion from a solid or liquid fuel-fired appliance to a chimney flue.

SOFFIT: Exposed horizontal underside of any architectural element such as a cornice or lintel.

STAIR LANDING: A platform between flights of stairs.

STENCILING: Painted decoration applied through a cut-out template to create a repeating pattern.

STILE: Vertical board used in framing or paneling, usually tenoned to fit into the mortises of the rails and grooved for the tongues of panels.

STOOL: The flat, narrow shelf forming the top member of the interior trim at the bottom of a window.

STOOP: A low platform with or without steps, outside the entrance door of a house.

STORM DOOR: An extra outside door for protection against inclement weather.

STRIKE PLATE: The part of a door–lock set that is fastened to the jamb.

STUD: 1. One of a series of wood structural components (usually of two-inch nominal thickness) used as supporting elements in walls and partitions. 2. A small vertical structural member inserted between the sill and plate forming the nailing surface for interior and exterior walls. 3. Intermediate posts between the main ones of a timber frame.

SUMMER BEAM: In early seventeenth and eighteenth century construction, the large wooden beam running from the chimney to the girder in the exterior structural frame.

SUMMER KITCHEN: A kitchen workroom where the cookstove was temporarily moved during the hottest summer months for kitchen comfort.

THRESHOLD: A strip of wood, metal, or other material beveled on each edge and used at the junction of two different floor finishes under doors, or on the top of the door sill at exterior doors.

THUMBNAIL BEAD: Quarter-round planed at the edge of a board, recessed slightly together from the surface from which it is cut; usually used on the stiles and rails of Georgian doors and fielded wall panels.

TIE-BEAM: Transverse horizontal beam at or near wall-top level, tying together the feet of the rafters and preventing their spread. It is above the wall plate in box-framed types of roof, below it in cruck construction.

TIMBER-FRAMED: Construction of a wooded skeleton with filling of wattle-and-daub, brick, etc.

TOENAILING: Nailing at an angle to the first member so as to ensure penetration into a second member.

TONGUE-AND-GROOVE: Method of joining wooden elements; the projecting tongue on one element is inserted into the groove of another element.

TONGUE-AND-GROOVE LUMBER: Any lumber, such as boards or planks, machined in such a way that there is a groove on one edge and a corresponding tongue on the other.

TRANSOM: A horizontal bar of wood or stone in window.

TREFOIL: A three-lobed pattern similar to a cloverleaf.

TRIM: Visible woodwork or molding of a building, including baseboards, moldings and casings, which cover joints, edges and ends of other materials.

TRUSS: Triangular framework with roof, to be self-supporting and carry other timbers, purlins, etc. These divide the building into bays.

VENEER: Thin pieces of wood, usually ornamental, used to cover inferior wood for decorative purposes or to add strength.

WAINSCOT: Facing, decorative or protective, for the lower portion of a wall, often of boards of panels. The term originally referred to quartered oak, then to boarding or paneling made of it, then sheathing or lining for walls.

WATTLE-AND-DAUB: Hurdlework or vertical stakes, interwoven with mixture of clay strengthened with straw, cow-hair, etc., and finished with plaster.

WEATHER-BOARDING: A series of horizontal boards set up on a sill, each overlapping the next, to throw off rain. The boards are wedge-shaped in section, the upper edge being the thinner.

WHITEWASH: Water-based paint made from ground chalk, salt and lime and sometimes tinted.

WHITING: Powdered calcium carbonate pigment, including ground chalk or clay, used in the composition of some paints such as whitewash.

Bibliography

Adam, Robert and James Adam. *The Works in Architecture of Robert and James Adam.* London: T. Beckett, 1773–74.

Bacon, H. Parrot. "History in Houses." *Antiques,* May 1983.

Briggs, Martin S. *The Homes of the Pilgrim Fathers in England and America (1620–1685).* London: Oxford University Press, 1932.

Brunskill, R.W. *Traditional Farm Buildings of Britain.* London: Victor Gallancz Ltd., 1982.

Byrne, Richard O., Jacques Lemire, Judy Oberlander, Gail Sussman and Martin Weaver. *Conservation of Wooden Monuments.* Heritage Canada Foundation, 1983.

Byrne, Richard O., editor. *The Victorian Design Book.* Ottawa: Lee Valley Tools Ltd., 1984.

Canadian Institute of Treated Wood. *Treated Wood Guidelines.* Ottawa: Canadian Institute of Treated Wood, 1989.

Central Mortgage and Housing Corporation. *Canadian Wood-Frame House Construction.* Ottawa: CMHC, 1968.

Charles, F.W.B. *Conservation of Timber Buildings.* London: Hutchinson & Co., 1984.

Downing, A.J. *The Architecture of Country Houses.* Revised edition. New York: Dover Publications, 1969.

Editors of the Early American Society. *Colonial Architecture in New England.* New England: Arno Press Inc., 1977.

Faulkner, Ann. *Without Our Past.* Toronto: University of Toronto Press, 1977.

Favretti, Rudy J. and Jory Putman Favretti. *Landscapes and Gardens for Historic Buildings.* Nashville, TN: American Association for State and Local History, 1978.

Findlay, W.P.K. *Timber: Properties and Uses.* London: Granada Publishing, 1975.

Fracchia, Charles A. and Jeremiah O. Bragstad. *Converted Into Houses.* London: Penguin Books, 1976.

Fram, Mark. *Well Preserved.* Erin, ON: Boston Mills Press, 1988.

Franklin, Wayne. *A Rural Carpenter's World.* Iowa City: University of Iowa Press, 1990.

Gerfin, W. *The Blacksmith.* Harrisburg, PN: Pennsylvania History and Museum Commission, 1976.

Gillis, Sandra J. *The Timber Trade in the Ottawa Valley.* Ottawa: Department of Indian and Northern Affairs (Parks Canada), 1975.

Girouard, Mark. *The Victorian Country House.* New Haven: Yale University Press, 1990.

Gowans, Alan. *Building Canada.* Toronto: Oxford University Press, 1966.

Hearn, John. *The Canadian Old House Catalogue.* Toronto: Van Nostrand Reinhold, 1980.

Hubka, Thomas C. *Big House, Little House, Back House, Barn: The Connected Farm Buildings of New England.* Hanover: University Press of New England, 1984.

Humphreys, Barbara and Meredith Sykes. *The Buildings of Canada.* Montreal: Reader's Digest Association (Canada), 1974.

Hutchins, Nigel and Donna Farron Hutchins. *Restoring Old Houses.* Toronto: Key Porter Books, 1997.

Hutchins, Nigel and Donna Farron Hutchins. *Restoring Houses of Brick and Stone.* Toronto: Key Porter Books, 1998.

Hutchinson, B.D., J. Barton and N. Ellis. *Maintenance and Repair of Buildings.* London: The Butterworth Group, 1975.

Insall, Donald W. *The Care of Old Buildings Today.* London: The Architectural Press, 1972.

Isham, Norman M. *A Glossary of Architectural Terms.* New York: American Life Foundation and Study Institute, 1978.

Jackson, Albert and David Day. *Woodworker's Manual.* London: HarperCollins, 1989.

Jandl, H. Ward, editor. *The Technology of Historic American Buildings.* Washington, D.C.: Foundation for Preservation Technology, 1983.

Johns, J. and G. Blumenson. *Identifying American Architecture.* Nashville: American Association for State and Local History, 1977.

Kalman, Harold. *The Sensible Rehabilitation of Older Houses.* Ottawa: Canada Mortgage and Housing Corporation, 1979.

Kimball, Fiske. *Domestic Architecture of the American Colonies and of the Early Republic.* New York: Dover Publications, 1922.

Langsner, Drew. *Green Woodworking.* Emmaus, PN: Rodale Press, 1987.

Lessard, Michel and Huguette Marquis. *Encyclopedie de la Maison Quebecoise.* Ottawa: Les Editions d'Homme, 1972.

Litchfield, Michael W. *Renovation: A Complete Guide.* New York: John Wiley & Sons, 1982.

London, Mark and Bumbaru Dinu. *Traditional Windows.* Montreal: Heritage Montreal, 1985.

Macrae, Marion. *The Ancestral Roof.* Toronto: Clarke, Irwin & Co., 1963.

Maguire, Byron W. *Carpentry for Residential Construction.* Reston, VA: Reston Publishing Co., 1975.

McAlester, Virginia and Lee McAlester. *A Field Guide to American Houses.* New York: Alfred A. Knopf, 1990.

McClintock, Mike. *Alternative Housebuilding.* New York: Sterling Publishing Co., 1945.

McRaven, Charles. *Building and Restoring the Hewn Log House.* Cincinnati, OH: Betterway Books, 1994.

Moogk, Peter N. *Building a House in New France.* Toronto: McClelland & Stewart, 1997.

Morrison, Hugh. *Early American Architecture.* New York: Oxford University Press, 1952.

Mullins, E.J. and T.S. McKnight. *Canadian Woods.* Toronto: University of Toronto Press, 1981.

New York Landmarks Conservancy. *Repairing Old and Historic Windows.* Washington, D.C.: The Preservation Press, 1992.

Phillips, Morgan W. and Judith E. Selwyn. *Epoxies for Wood Repairs in Historic Buildings.* Washington, D.C.: Office of Archaeology and Historic Preservation, 1978.

Phillips, Steven I. *Old House Dictionary.* Washington, D.C.: The Preservation Press, 1994.

Pierson, William H. Jr. *American Buildings and Their Architects.* New York: Doubleday, 1978.

Rawson, Marion Nicholl. *Sing Old House.* New York: E.P. Dutton, 1934.

Rempel, John I. *Building with Wood.* Toronto: University of Toronto Press, 1967.

Shivers, Natalie. *Walls & Moulding: How to Care for Old and Historic Wood and Plaster.* Washington, D.C.: The Preservation Press, 1990.

Smith, Baird M. *Conserving Energy in Historic Buildings.* Washington, D.C.: Office of Archaeology and Historic Preservation, 1978.

Sprague, Dr. Paul E. *Technology of Historic American Buildings.* ???

Strickland, Samuel. *Twenty-Seven Years in Canada West, or, The Experience of an Early Settler.* Agnes Strickland, editor. London: R. Bentley, 1853.

Underwood, Grahame and John Planck. *A Handbook of Architectural Ironmongery.* London: Architectural Press, 1977.

Wagner, Willis H. *Modern Carpentry.* South Holland, Illinois: Goodheart-Wilcox Co., 1976.

Wagner, Willis H. *Modern Woodworking.* South Holland, Illinois: Goodheart-Wilcox Co., 1974.

Weaver, Martin R. *The Conservation of Wood in Historic Buildings.* Ottawa: Department of Northern and Indian Affairs, 1978.

Wilcox, Wayne, Elmer E. Botsai and Hans Kubler, *Wood as a Building Material.* New York: Wiley–Interscience Publishing, 1991.

Wills, James T. "Living with Antiques." *Antiques,* June 1983.

Wood, Margaret. *The English Mediaeval House.* London: Bracken Books, 1983.

Zimell, Umberto and Giovanni Vergerio. *Decorative Ironwork.* London: Hamlyn Publishing Group, 1969.

Additional Resources

Associations

Association for the Preservation of Technology Intl.
Box 8178
Fredericksburg, VA 22044
(540) 373-1621/fax: (540) 373-6050

The Canadian Association of Professional Heritage
Consultants
P.O. Box 1023, Station F
Toronto, Ontario M4Y 2T7
Fax: (416) 763-4082

Heritage Canada Foundation
412 MacLaren
Ottawa, Ontario K2P 0M8
(613) 237-1066 or 237-1867/fax: (613) 237-5987
e-mail: hercanot@sympatico.ca

Heritage Canada, National Office
P.O. Box 1358, Station B
Ottawa, Ontario K1P 5R4
(613) 237-1066/fax: (613) 237-5987

National Trust for Historic Preservation
1785 Massachusetts N.W.
Washington, DC 20036
(202) 588-6000/fax: (202) 588-6038
website: www.nhtp.ort

Ontario Heritage Foundation
10 Adelaide St. East
Toronto, Ontario M5C 1J3
(416) 325-5000/fax: (416) 325-5000

Regional Offices, Heritage Canada

Heritage Canada, Atlantic Canada
P.O. Box 2024, Station M
Halifax, Nova Scotia B3J 2Z1
(902) 421-1889/fax: (902) 423-8808

Heritage Canada, Bureau du Quebec
11, rue Ancie Chantier
Quebec, Quebec G1K 6T4
(418) 694-9944/fax: (418) 694-9488

Heritage Canada, Ontario Office
59 Dickson, Suite 282
Cambridge, Ontario N1R 1T5
(519) 622-3036/fax: (519) 622-3036

Heritage Canada, Western Office
Suite 150, 105 21st Street East
Saskatoon, Saskatchewan S7K 0B3
(306) 934-3622/fax: (306) 652-9292

Regional Offices, National Trust

Mid-Atlantic Regional Office
6401 Germantown Avenue
Philadelphia, PA 19144

Midwest Regional Office
53 West Jackson Boulevard, Suite 1135
Chicago, IL 60604

Mountains/Plains Regional Office
511 16th Street, Suite 700
Denver, CO 80202

Northeast Regional Office
Old City Hall
45 School Street, 4th floor
Boston, MA 02108

Southern Regional Office
456 King St.
Charleston, SC 29403

Texas/New Mexico Field Office
500 Main Street, Suite 606
Fort Worth, TX 76102

Western Regional Office
One Sutter Street, Suite 707
San Francisco, CA 94104

MAGAZINES AND REFERENCE BOOKS

Century Home Magazine
12 Mill Street South
Port Hope, Ontario L1A 2S5
(905) 885-9687/fax: (905) 885-5355

Colonial Homes
1790 Broadway
New York, NY 10019
(212) 830-2900/fax: (212) 586-3455

Historic Preservation
National Trust for Historic Preservation
748 Jackson Place N.W.
Washington, DC 20006

The Old House Journal/Old House Interiors
Dovetale Publishers
The Blackburn Tavern
2 Main Street
Gloucester, MA 01930
(508) 283-3200/1-800-234-3797 **OHJ** only
1-800-462-0211 **OHI** only

SCHOOLS AND WORKSHOPS

Algonquin College
Museum Technology Program
1385 Woodroffe Avenue
Nepean, Ontario K2E 5L2
(613) 727-4723

Algonquin College
Perth, Ontario
(613) 735-4712

Eastfield Village
P.O. Box 145
East Nassau, NY 12062

International Centre for the Study of the Preservation of
Cultural Property (ICCROM)
13 Via di San Michele
Rome, Italy 00153

Restore Skills Training Program
30 Rockefeller Plaza
New York, NY 10020

TOOLS

Lee Valley Tools
1080 Morrison Drive
Ottawa, Ontario K2H 8K7
(613) 596-0350/fax: (613) 596-3073

Lee Valley Tools
5511 Steeles West
Toronto, Ontario M9O 1S7
(416) 746-0850/fax: (416) 746-8474

Woodcraft Supply Corporation
313 Montvale Avenue
Woburn, MA 01801
(617) 935-6414/fax: (617) 935-6454

Woodcraft Supply Corporation
210 Wood County Industrial Park
P.O. Box 1686
Parkersburg, VA 26012
Tech. Advice: (304) 464-1074/1-800-225-1153
Fax order: (304) 428-8271

Further Readings

ARCHITECTURE

Adam, Robert and James Adam. *The Works in Architecture of Robert and James Adam.* London: T. Becket, 1773-74.

Bicknell, A.J., and William T. Comstock. *Victorian Architecture: Two Pattern Books.* Watkins Glen, New York: Atheneum Publishers, 1976.

Blumenson, John G. *Identifying American Architecture.* Nashville, Tennessee: American Association for State and Local History, 1977.

Burden, Ernest. *Living Barns.* New York: New York Graphic Society Books, 1977.

Clarke, Harold. *Georgian Dublin.* Dublin: Eason and Son, 1976.

Davey, Andy, et al. *Architecture: Nineteenth and Twentieth Centuries.* Edinburgh: Paul Harris Publishing, 1978

———. *The Care and Conservation of Georgian Houses.* Edinburgh: Paul Harris Publishing, 1978.

Downing, A.J. *The Architecture of Country Houses.* New York: Dover Publications, 1969.

Faulkner, Ann. *Without Our Past.* Toronto: University of Toronto Press, 1977.

Gilliat, Mary. *English Style.* London: Bodley Head, 1967.

Girouard, Mark. *The Victorian Country House.* New Haven: Yale University Press, 1979.

———. *The English Town: A History of Urban Life.* New Haven: Yale University Press, 1990.

Gowans, Alan. *Building Canada.* Toronto: Oxford University Press, 1966.

Hubka, Thomas C. *Big House, Little House, Back House, Barn: The Connected Farm Buildings of New England.* Hanover: University Press of New England, 1984.

Humphreys, Barbara and Merideth Sykes. *The Buildings of Canada.* Montreal: Reader's Digest Association, Canada, 1974.

Isham, Norman M. *A Glossary of Architectural Terms.* New York: American Life Foundation and Study Institute, 1978.

Kimball, Fiske. *Domestic Architecture of the American Colonies and of the Early Republic.* New York: Dover Publications, 1922.

Lasdun, Susan. *Victorians at Home.* New York: The Viking Press, 1981.

Late Victorian Architectural Details. Watkins Glen, New York: American Life Foundation and Study Institute, 1978.

Lessard, Michel, and Huguette Marquis. *Encyclopédie de la maison Quebécoise.* Ottawa: Les Editions de l'Homme, 1972.

Macrae, Marion. *The Ancestral Roof.* Toronto: Clarke, Irwin & Company, 1963.

McAlester, Virginia, and Lee McAlester. *A Field Guide to American Houses.* New York: Alfred A. Knopf, 1990.

Mercer, Henry C. *The Dating of Old Houses.* Watkins Glen, New York: American Life Foundation and Study Institute, 1978.

Norberg-Schulz, Christian. *The Concept of Dwelling: On the Way to Figurative Architecture.* New York: Electa/Rizzoli, 1993.

Phillips, R.A.J. *Up the Streets of Ontario.* Ottawa: Heritage Canada, 1976.

Pierson, William H., Jr. *American Buildings and Their Architects.* New York: Doubleday and Company, 1978.

Richardson, Douglas. *Architecture in Ontario.* Toronto: Ontario Ministry of Culture and Recreation, 1976.

Rothery, Sean. *Everyday Building of Ireland.* Dublin: College of Technology, 1975.

Shivers, Natalie. *Walls & Molding: How to Care for Old and Historic Wood and Plaster.* The Preservation Press, 1990.

Stokes, Peter John. *Old Niagara-on-the-Lake.* Toronto: University of Toronto Press, 1971.

Tallmadge, Thomas E. *The Story of Architecture in America.* New York: W.W. Norton & Co., 1936.

Von Rosenstiel, Helene, and Gail Caskey Winkler. *Floor Coverings for Historic Building: A Guide to Selecting Reproductions.* The Preservation Press, 1988.

CONSTRUCTION

Ashurst, John, and Francis G. Dimes. *Stone Building: Its Use and Potential Today.* Lond: Architectural Press, 1977.

Blackburn, Graham. *Illustrated Housebuilding.* Woodstock, New York: Overlook Press, 1974.

Blackwell, Duncan S. *The Complete Book of Outdoor Masonry.* Pennsylvania: Tab Books, 1978.

Ching, Francis D.K. *Building Construction Illustrated.* New York: Van Nostrand Reinhold, 1975.

Clidero, Robert K. and Kenneth H. Sharpe. *Applications of Electrical Construction.* Don Mills, Ontario: General Publishing, 1975.

Complete Do-It-Yourself Manual. Montreal: Reader's Digest Association, 1973.

Maguire, Byron W. *Carpentry for Residential Construction.* Reston, Virginia: Reston Publishing Co., 1975.

Plastering Skill and Practice. Chicago: American Technical Society, 1978.

Vivian, John. *Building Stone Walls.* Vermont: Greeway Publishing, 1976.

Wagner, Willis H. *Modern Carpentry.* South Holland, Illinois: Goodheart-Wilcox Co., 1976.

———-. *Modern Woodworking.* South Holland, Illinois: Goodheart-Wilcox Co., 1974.

HEATING

Keeping the Heat In. Ottawa: Energy, Mines and Resources Canada, 1976.

Kurka, Norma S. and Jan Naar. *Design for a Limited Planet: Living with Natural Energy.* New York: Ballantine Books, 1976.

Rumford, Count. *Essays: Political, Economical and Philosophical.* London, 1795.

Smith, Baird M. "Conserving Energy in Historic Buildings," *Preservation Briefs,* no. 3, U.S. Department of the Interior, April 1978, pp. 1-8.

Vivian, John. *Wood Heat.* Emmaus, Pennsylvania: Rodale Press, 1976.

IRON

Gerfin, W. *The Blacksmith.* Harrisburg, Pennsylvania: Pennsylvania History and Museum Commission, 1976.

Sloane, Eric. *A Museum of Early American Tools.* New York: Ballantine Books, 1973.

Underwood, Grahame, and John Planck. *A Handbook of Architectural Ironmongery.* London: Architectural Press, 1977.

Zimelli, Umberto and Giovanni Vergerio. *Decorative Ironwork.* London: Hamlyn Publishing Group, 1969.

LANDSCAPE

Favrietti, Rudy J. and Joy Putman Favretti. *Landscapes and Gardens for Historic Buildings.* Nashville, Tennessee: American Association for State and Local History, 1978.

McHarg, Ian L. *Design with Nature.* Garden City, New York: Doubleday & Co., 1969.

Stewart, John J. "Historic Landscapes and Gardens," *Technical Leaflet 80*, American Association for State and Local History (November 1974), pp. 32-48.

LIGHTING

Hayward, Arthur H. *Colonial and Early American Lighting.* Toronto: Dover Publications, 1962.

Myers, Denys Peter. Gas *Lighting in America: A Guide for Historic Preservation.* Washington, D.C.: U.S. Department of the Interior, 1978.

Westinghouse Lighting Handbook. Dorval, Quebec: Westinghouse Canada, 1976.

PAINTS & WALLPAPERS

Frangiamore, Catherine Lynn. *Wallpapers in Historic Preservation.* Washington, D.C.: U.S. Department of the Interior, Technical Preservation Services Division, Office of Archaelogy and Historic Preservation, National Park Service, 1977.

Minhinnick, Jeanne. "Some Personal Observations on the Use of Paint in Early Ontario," *Association for the Preservation of Technology,* vol. vii, no. 2 (1975), p. 13.

Waring, Janet. *Early American Stencil Decorations.* Watkins Glen, New York: Century House, 1937.

Welsh, Frank S. "A Methodology for Exposing and Preserving Architectural Graining," *Association for the Preservation of Technology,* vol. viii, no. 2 (1976), p. 71.

Zirkle, John F. "The Refinishing Clinic: A Whitewash Formula," *The Old House Journal* (September 1979), p. 107.

Zucker, Howard. "Graining," *The Old House Journal* (June 1975), pp. 10-22.

PRESERVATION

Bullock, Orin M. *The Restoration Manual.* Norwalk, Connecticut: Silvermin Publishers, 1966.

Cobb, Hubbard H. *How to Buy and Remold the Older House.* New York: Collier Books, 1965.

Finley, Gerald. *In Praise of Older Buildings.* Kingston, Ontario: Frontenac Historic Foundation, 1976.

Fracchia, Charles A. and Jeremiah O. Bragstad. *Converted Into Houses.* London: Penguin Books, 1976.

Galt, George. *Investing in the Past: A Report on the Profitability of Heritage Conservation.* Ottawa: Heritage Canada, 1974.

Guidelines for Rehabilitating Old Buildings. Washington, D.C.: U.S. Department of Housing and Urban Development, 1977.

Haynes, Robert E. *A Bibliography of Historic Preservation.* Washington, D.C.: National Park Service, 1977.

Hearn, John. *The Canadian Old House Catalogue.* Toronto: Van Nostrand Reinhold, 1980.

Insall, Donald W. *The Care of Old Buildings Today.* London: The Architectural Press, 1972.

Little, Nina Fletcher. *Floor Coverings in New England Before 1850.* Norwalk, Connecticut: Old Sturbridge, 1967.

Litchfield, Michael W. *Renovation: A Complete Guide.* New York: John Wiley & Sons, 1982.

Mack, Robert C. "The Cleaning and Waterproof Coating of Masonry Buildings," *Preservation Brief No. 1,* U.S. Department of the Interior, April 1978, pp. 1-4.

———. *Repointing Mortar Joints in Historic Buildings.* Washington, D.C.: National Park Service, 1976.

McKee, Harley J. *Introduction to Early American Masonry.* Washington, D.C.: Columbia University Press, 1973.

The Old House Journal Catalog. New York: The Old House Journal Corporation, 1979.

Papian, William N. "Insulation in Old Houses," *The Old House Journal,* August 1976 (part 1), pp. 14-23; September 1976 (part 2), pp. 31-43.

Phillips, Morgan W. and Judith E. Selwyn. *Epoxies for Wood Repairs in Historic Buildings.* Washington, D.C.: Office of Archeology and Historic Preservation, 1978.

Prudon, Theodore H.M. "Wooden Structural Members: Some Recent European Preservation Methods," *Association for the Preservation of Technology,* vol. iii, no. 1 (1975), p. 5.

Rawson, Marion Nicholl. *Sing Old House.* New York: E.P. Dutton, 1934.

Stephen, George. *Remodeling Old Houses.* New York: Alfred A. Knopf, 1974.

Stumes, Paul. "The Application of Eopxy Results for the Restoration of Historic Structures," *Association for the Preservation of Technology,* vol. iii, no. 1 (1975), p. 6.

Watson, Joyce N. "Tracing the History of a House," *Ontario Library Review,* March 1976, pp. 82-96.

Weaver, Martin R. *The Conservation of Wood in Historic Buildings.* Ottawa: Department of Indian and Northern Affairs, 1978.

ROOMS

Conran, Terrance. *The Bed and Bath Book.* New York: Crown Publishers, 1978.

———. *The Kitchen Book.* New York: Crown Publishers, 1977.

Phipps, Frances. *Colonial Kitchens: Their Furnishings and Their Gardens.* New York: Hawthorn Books, 1972.

Ribalta, Marta, ed. *Habitat: El Dormitoro—The Bedroom—La Chambre à Coucher.* Barcelona: Editorial Blume, 1975.

———. *Habitat: La Salle de Estor—The Livingroom—La Salle de Séjour.* Barcelona: Editorial Blume, 1975.

GENERAL

Crawford, Patricia. *Homesteading: A Practical Guide to Living Off the Land.* New York: Collier Macmillan Co., 1975.

Guillet, Edwin C. *Pioneer Arts and Crafts.* Toronto: University of Toronto, 1968.

Kalm, Peter. *Travels in North America.* Warrington, England: n. pub., 1812.

McGill, Jean S. *A Pioneer History of the County of Lanark.* Toronto: self-published, 1968.

McKendry, Ruth. *Quilts and Other Bed Coverings in the Canadian Tradition.* Toronto: Van Nostrand Reinhold, 1979.

Minhinnick, Jeanne. *At Home in Upper Canada.* Toronto: Clarke, Irwin & Company, 1970.

Moodie, Susanna. *Roughing It in the Bush, or Forest Life in Canada.* Toronto: Bell & Cockburn, 1913.

Nutting, Wallace. *Furniture of the Pilgrim Century.* New York: Dover Publications, 1965.

———. *Furniture Treasury.* New York: The Macmillan Co., 1928.

Pain, Howard. *The Heritage of Upper Canadian Furniture.* Toronto: Van Nostrand Reinhold, 1978.

Palardy, Jean. *The Furniture of French Canada.* Toronto: Macmillan Co. of Canada, 1963.

Spence, Hilda and Kelvin Spence. *A Guide to Early Canadian Glass.* Don Mills, Ontario: Longmans, 1966.

Stevens, Gerald. *Early Ontario Glass.* Toronto: University of Toronto Press, 1965.

De Uries, Leonard and Ilonka van Amstel. *The Wonderful World of American Advertisements.* London: John Murray, 1972.

Wurtele, F.C. "Historical Records of the St. Maurice Forges," *Transactions of the Royal Society of Canada,* vol. 4, sec. II, pp. 77-89.

Index

adobe, 17

balloon framing, 19, 22, 30, 32
base board, 107
board and batten, 95, 97–98
braced framing, 19, 22, 30
bridging, 57

carpenter ants, 70
caulking, 89
clob, 14
clapboard siding, 19, 95, 97
clapholy, 19
columbage pierotté, 28
color window, 125–127
condensation, 119
cornice, 76, 79, 83, 90

death watch beetle, 68
diagonal bracing, 19
distemper, 131
dry rot, 67–68

fanlight, 83
fencing, 152–153, 157
floors, 106–107
foundation, 56, 60, 61
frass, 66
froe, 23
fungi, 66–68

George Washington Snow, 32
girts, 19

glass, 95
glazing, 87–88
grinning, 144
guttering, 63

hardware, 113–114, 120
Holmes, James C., 32

infill, 28
insulation, 117–118
Italianate, 54

jacking, 66
Jamestown, Virginia, 14
joinery, 106
joists, 19, 20

keystone, 83

landscape, 151
lap joints, 19, 24
lath, 110
log houses, 33, 98–100, 102
longhouse, 14

Magnolia Mount Plantation, 30
maison au columbage, 28
mantel, 115–116
mechanical systems, 117
moisture content, 85
moisture meter, 85
moldings, 112

nails, 110–111
neo-Classical, 106
neo-Gothic, 44

panel, 107
parging, 13
partitions, 107
period paint, 139–143, 147
photo documentation, 48
piece sur piece, 30
pit saw, 28
plates, 19, 20
porch, 91
posts, 19
primeval, 17
principal rafters, 19
purlins, 19

rafters, 19, 21, 78, 79, 80
ridge pole, 19

sagging, 144
sash, 86–88
sawmill, 28
sheathing, 19
shingle, 74, 90
shutters, 91, 95
sills, 19
soffit and fascia, 53
staircase, 115
Ste. Marie Among the Hurons, 28
Strickland, Samuel, 23
strippers, 127, 128

stud wall, 109
summer beam, 19–20

timber framing, 17, 19, 30, 32
toxic woods, 145

underpinning, 58

vapor barrier, 116

wainscot, 122
wattle and daub, 14–15
weeping tile, 55, 59, 61
western framing, 19, 33
White Swan Tavern, 50

whitewash, 129
window, 91
wood finishing, 133–138
wood preservative, 68

About the Authors

Nigel John Hutchins is a respected authority on the preservation of old buildings. In addition to this book, he is the author of two companion volumes, *Restoring Houses of Brick and Stone* and *Restoring Old Houses.*

Hutchins acquired a commercial art diploma and studied set design at Montreal's National Theatre School. His interest in architectural conservation began in the early 1970s while he was restoring a log house for use in a feature film. He has received numerous awards for his contribution to the restoration and preservation of over 90 conservation projects, and was heritage consultant to the Ontario Building Code Commission for two terms. He frequently lectures at colleges, historical societies, and preservation conferences.

Donna Farron Hutchins is a psychotherapist in private practice in Southwestern Ontario. Her background includes twenty years as a professional actress and artist. Her knowledge of the sociological context of domestic architecture and her enthusiasm for research played a pivotal role in the process of writing this book.